THE POTENTIAL OF MEDIUMSHIP

Glyn Edwards

The Potential of

MEDIUMSHIP

Expanded Edition

**A Collection of
Essential Teachings and Exercises**

*Compiled and with an introduction by
Santoshan (Stephen Wollaston)*

❖

Published by S Wollaston, 2017
Independent publishing platform

Copyright © 2017 Glyn Edwards and Santoshan (Stephen Wollaston)

ISBN:
979-8479718465 (hardback) / 978-0956921031 (paperback)
3rd edition (expanded edition)
Amazon hardback 2021 / paperback 2020
(back cover compiler information updated in 2024)

A CIP record of this book is available from the British Library

The Potential of Mediumship is an anthology of
new and previously published material by Glyn Edwards,
compiled and edited by Santoshan (Stephen Wollaston) with permission
from the author for the original first and second edition.
Permission was given to include extra material by the family of the author
for this expanded edition. The first edition was published by
the Gordon Higginson Fellowship in 2012.

Design, artwork and back cover photo by Santoshan (Stephen Wollaston)
Front cover and title page image © Agsandrew/Shutterstock.com

Back cover photo taken in East London, 2001.
Afterword photo of the compiler and Glyn Edwards,
taken on Malaga Beach, Spain, in 1989.

Page 125 upated in 2026.

Contents

Dedicated to Vi and Eddie
and to Pat and Dave

Preface
About the Expanded Edition

Since the release of the first edition of *The Potential of Mediumship*, Glyn made that transition which we will all have to make one day to spirit. Because of this, it seems fitting to include a more detailed biography about him than before in this extended version of the book. It should perhaps be mentioned that Glyn was never interested in having a *biographical book* put together about him, so placing something more modest in breadth in this anthology of his wisdom seems more of a logical thing to do in memory of him.

As well as the added information about Glyn, this edition also includes two additional articles he dictated shortly after the first version of the book was published, which are two of just a few final articles he did not long before his passing. The added articles have been deliberately placed at the end as appendices so as not to change the main order of the chapters from the first edition. Hopefully, readers will find the new material a beneficial addition.

If we accept that life is eternal and there are other realms of existence intertwined with our physical world, then it must be a natural step in our evolution to be able to communicate with these other realms and with those who are living on.

When approached in a healthy way, we discover that mediumistic unfoldment is an active and evolving path that leads to new and profound experience and deep contact with the world of the spirit.

~ GLYN EDWARDS

Introduction

I knew Glyn as a close friend for 26 years. In those years, we somehow managed to find some time to work on three books together and work on the first edition of this anthology of his teachings and collection of exercises he used to help students move forward with their abilities and potential growth.

Some passages in this anthology are from the books that we jointly worked on.* Others are from an article he did especially for the Gordon Higginson Fellowship website, an organisation Glyn founded, from discussions with him about extra sections that could be included, and from one of his many audio recordings. There is one place where Glyn asked for a paragraph I had written to be included, which has been put in italics to distinguish it from Glyn's words. If you wish to know the sources used for each chapter, they have been listed towards the end of this book.

This book is of course by no means an exhaustive collection of *everything* Glyn had to say or wrote on the

---

*Although the main parts of our first book were credited with joint authorship, as we worked on each other's material and coauthored some chapters, Glyn and I obviously knew which parts were his and could be used in this anthology.

subject of the Potential of Mediumship, but it is the very first anthology of different works by him to be published on the topic. Unlike standard books of quotations that layout what people have written or said without making alterations, some creative editing was done. As Glyn was actively involved in every stage of the original book's formation, selecting which passages to include, deciding how best to fit numerous sections together, and even did some light editing himself, we both felt some creative editing would be acceptable and beneficial in weaving various sections together in order to present the essential message of the quoted sources in a readable style. We also wanted the book to have its own uniqueness, which was the reason behind adding new material, including some personal stories of Glyn's.

Glyn's teachings

In all the years I knew Glyn, he always read widely and took a deep interest in numerous contemporary fields of spirituality, different religious beliefs, various forms of healing and modern discoveries in science and psychology. He also loved engaging in open and beneficial dialogues with people from different traditions. Naturally, his interests in wide approaches to spirituality and mediumship are detectable in his writings.

Readers will notice that Glyn's teachings on mediumship promote a fresh contemporary perspective. He did not see *any abilities* we have as being separate from anything else. His teachings are essentially an affirmation and holistic inclusion of all life, instead of a denial of some aspects as some teachers and different traditions have promoted. He taught about an ongoing evolvement and exploration into how all things continuously interrelate with each other. This was never about a belief in having all the answers, which in fact inhibits development, but about being open to growth at all times. Although his writings sometimes use terms such as 'path', 'journey' or 'quest', they are not so much about *going someplace else* but about deepening understanding of the spirit world that is present now and in all things. Even though he mentions the importance of transcendence at times, he never sees it as escaping from Earth life but including it and recognising how spiritual realms are essentially interwoven with our physical world.

He often took mediumship out of its box in order to integrate it with the collective responsibilities we share for each other and the natural world, which is comparable in many ways to Shamanistic understandings of spirituality and spirit contact.

As a writer and member of GreenSpirit, I find Glyn's teachings to be deeply encouraging, as they take the subject of mediumship beyond being purely *human-centred* – either in this life or in the afterlife – and are integrated with an active *Gaia-centred* spirituality that is crucial at this moment in the history of the world for the survival of so many of God's creatures and the conservation of important ecosystems. For Glyn, all life and phenomena are seen as expressions of the creativity of the spirit that is forever seeking to encourage us to awaken more authentically, compassionately, widely and actively to our spiritual natures and to what knowledge of an eternal existence implies.

When I first completed this collection of teachings and exercises by Glyn, I couldn't help noticing how it in some ways read like a meditations book. Not only because of the exercises included but also because Glyn's words present us with profound perspectives on which to reflect in order to uncover deeper dimensions of life and living.

I hope you will find much food for replenishment in the following pages. May the paths you explore be blessed with love and wisdom and lead you to ever-present life changing dimensions of spiritual growth and to the infinite variety of gifts that can unfold, including, as Glyn reminds us, the gifts of friendship, compassion, understanding and unity with Nature and the world of the spirit that is continuously seeking harmonious expression through all.

~ SANTOSHAN (STEPHEN WOLLASTON)

Glyn Edwards

*In the course of my development I have come to realise how
our individual spirit, Nature, the spirit world and God are
continuously creating, and how by participating with this
activity we become co-creators with the creative powers of all life.*
~ GLYN EDWARDS

G lyn Edwards was born in Liverpool on 17th
August 1949 and was the oldest of four siblings.
His parents, Violet and Eddie, came from Catholic
and Welsh Presbyterian Church backgrounds. As Glyn's
father was in the army, Glyn spent a lot of his early years
living in different parts of the world such as Cyprus and
Egypt. His parents then settled for a while in the UK
when Eddie, with Violet's help, became a pub landlord in
Aylesbury, Buckinghamshire. They then lived in the United
States for a period, but Glyn remained in England.

During his Earth life, Glyn became internationally recognised as one of the UK's finest mediums. At 16 he joined a Benedictine community. Within this period of his life, various mediumistic experiences he had had since a child intensified, which subsequently led him to leave the community after staying for two years. He then went on to train at Sassoon's, became a sought-after hairdresser and began to take a deeper interest in his mediumistic abilities after a sitting under an assumed name with a medium who gave him remarkable evidence about his gandmother and other members of his family.

After doing his first public demonstration of mediumship at 19, he immediately went on to working regularly as a medium. He later became a certificated medium of the SNU (Spiritualists' National Union) and a protégée of the world-renowned medium Gordon M Higginson, and worked on a variety of projects with him for many years, including demonstrating his mediumship at the Derby Assembly Rooms in 1991 as part of the SNU's centenary celebrations.

He travelled extensively, speaking, lecturing, demonstrating and running workshops throughout the UK and worldwide for over 40 years. He owed much of his early work to Jean Matheson, a long-time friend and organiser of numerous successful events and courses in the north of England, who sat for him in a highly productive development circle and helped him gain confidence in his abilities.

He was the main founder of the Gordon Higginson Fellowship and the Gordon Higginson Awareness Foundation, both of which ran various courses in the south of

England. He was also a regular course organiser and teacher at the Arthur Findlay College for over three decades, worked at the Spiritualist Association of Great Britain, and was involved with the research of PRISM (Psychical Research Involving Selected Mediums).

He possessed extensive understanding of various mediumistic and spiritual paths, and was always up-to-date with the latest ideas and discoveries of different traditions. He was particularly known for the quality of his work and his ability to demonstrate his mediumship almost effortlessly in front of large audiences. A short YouTube video of Glyn publicly demonstrating his mediumship, taken from a documentary shown on the BBC about the SNU, shows him giving evidence that even the most hardened sceptic would find difficult to explain away about a town where someone used to live having 'a very unusual post box', as it wasn't painted red, 'it was green and made out of wood'!

On some occasions he gave a demonstration of trance mediumship. More than anything, Glyn was highly respected for his understanding of and insight into different areas of mediumistic unfoldment and his devotion to helping students explore and realise their individual potential. His teachings and courses often promoted an inclusive approach to development. Along with those from Spiritualist backgrounds, students and teachers on his courses and workshops could come from a variety of traditions such as Hindu, Christian, Jewish, Yogic, Buddhist, Sufi, Psychotherapist, Reiki Healer and Neo-Pagan, and could be of any age from teenage years to senior citizens.

He was interviewed on television and radio throughout the world, recorded many teachings and practices, wrote numerous articles on mediumship and spiritual growth, and coauthored two development manuals (*Tune in to Your Spiritual Potential* and *21 Steps to Reach Your Spirit*). Because of other commitments Glyn had and the slow process of publishing in the 90s, the first book took eight years from conception to being released in printed form. Nonetheless, Glyn worked on several of his chapters while on a single two week holiday in the New Forest area in south England. The two coauthored books were thoroughly revised and given new titles in 2011: *The Spirit World in Plain English* and *Spirit Gems*. Glyn was also extensively featured in two in-depth interviews in the book *Realms of Wondrous Gifts*, released in 2008, and featured in a book called *The Best of British*, which was released to coincide with the new millennium.

In order to recharge his own batteries, Glyn frequently went on silent retreats to various countryside and town monasteries in the UK. For a while, he undertook instruction from a renowned tantric yoga master, Sri Jammu Maharaj, as well as a teacher from the Bihar School of Yoga, Swami Dharmananda Saraswati Maharaj, who gave him the name Devadasa (meaning 'servant of God'). Along with Eastern wisdom and practices such as Mindfulness, Glyn was for many years deeply inspired by the teachings of the New Thought writer and teacher Ernest Holmes, took serious interest in the revival of Centring Prayer pioneered by Thomas Keating, and found times being amongst Nature an important part of his spiritual life. Two of his favourite places to go on holiday were the Lake District in the north of England, and Devon in the south. Insights about the creativity of Nature, an ever-present spirit world and the Divinity in all were often predominant themes in Glyn's talks and writings.

He had a deep passion for reading about different spiritual paths; his modest apartment in Maids Moreton, Buckinghamshire was like a wonderful library of universal wisdom. He also had a great love of art, live theatre, poetry, and various styles of music, particularly the joyousness that is often expressed in JS Bach's compositions, and the sublime vocal skills of the Indian singer Kaushiki Chakrabarty. Both Bach and Chakrabarty were often found to be playing more than any other CDs on Glyn's car stereo.

In 2003 he made the front page of Psychic News (which he had done many times in his mediumistic life) after being struck-down by a mystery illness that affected the muscles on the left side of his face as well as his balance and often used a stick for walking from then on. After this, he showed how determination and the power of the spirit can overcome adversity. Remarkably, many testified to how his work and teachings moved on to a deeper level. He personally found this chapter in his life opening up many profound insights and experiences that expanded his mediumistic and spiritual understanding.

In the late spring of 2014 he was diagnosed with cancer and underwent chemotherapy. Although it became clear Glyn was not responding well to the treatment, he insisted on teaching up to the last and even began an outline for an article from his hospital bed towards the end of his Earth life. He remained positive and passed to spirit peacefully with his mother and sister, Elaine, by his side at 10 am on 31st May 2015. A service for close friends and family was held in the morning at Crownhill Crematorium, Milton Keynes, on 12th June. A celebration of his life was especially held in the afternoon at Akeley Village Hall for public attendance and to coincide with his youngest brother, Delwyn, and one of Glyn's best friends being in the UK at the same time.

People whose lives had been touched by Glyn came from as far as Scotland, Germany, Sweden and Holland. Ian Mowll, an Interfaith minister, led the afternoon celebration, during which family members, respected mediums and close friends of Glyn's such as Eileen Davies and Mark Stone shared treasured memories about him. Other celebration and memorial services and remembrances of Glyn's life were also organised, including one at the Greater Boston Church of Spiritualism in the United States, and one by the SNU at the Arthur Findlay College on its Open Week in 2016, which was written about in Psychic News and accompanied by an article about Glyn, his life, loves and individual spiritual growth.

Glyn's work lives on of course in his books, recordings and with various people and students he helped, many of whom have become teachers and mediums because of Glyn's help. There have even been reports of him communicating via some working mediums and mediumistic development circles.

Realms of
Unfoldment

1

M any years ago I gave a demonstration of mediumship at a Spiritualist Church in the Midlands. I began by giving information from a spirit communicator to a woman near the front of the congregation. I mentioned that this lady's mother was starting to communicate with me and that she was telling me how their relationship with each other was one of equal respect and friendship.

Whilst giving this information I found myself suddenly overwhelmed by a deep love the mother felt for her daughter, which was one of authentic support and not a love that smothered or sought to control. The woman receiving this information agreed. As this information was accepted, the love and presence of the mother intensified. Because of my inexperience in the art of mediumship at that time I felt that if the contact with the woman's mother continued to affect me in the way it was, I would not be able to continue the communication.

What I realise now is that the love I had become aware of coming from the mother was simply her drawing close to me as the medium and expressing her desire to establish evidential communication with her daughter. After the demonstration, the medium Gordon Higginson, who had been chairing the meeting, spoke to me about the need to trust mediumistic communication and no matter what, to continue as best as I could to establish *why the communicator had come*, thereby strengthening my contact with the spirit world and working with those who sought to communicate with and through me.

Like any setbacks in our development there was of course a lesson to be learned through this, which was about trusting the spirit and realising that our contact with their world is an opportunity to explore mediumistic abilities instead of being defeated by beliefs that could hinder their communication. We need to remember that nothing happens by chance. It is by being open to the many realms of mediumship that we open ourselves to different types of unfoldment and numerous spheres of spirit communication.

I have found that as I have awakened to various potentials of my mediumistic abilities, it has opened up many doors to a wider understanding of life and of how the spirit world is a part of everything and everyone. This has happened quite naturally by not being too quick to conceptualise and categorise various experiences and phenomena into rigid frameworks that would set me apart from people with other beliefs and abilities, which would have limited the enriching paths of mediumistic unfoldment I have undertaken.

What follows are some central facets that I both feel and believe are important to consider in mediumship. But I would not wish you to take these on board without reflecting upon them and deciding for yourself their use and validity. Ultimately the responsibility for your growth lies in your own hands. Though any effort you are prepared to make will put into operation the law of cause and effect, as well as the law of attraction and association, which will bring about corresponding changes that will draw those of similar minds to work with you.

None of this implies achieving some kind of ego-centred idealised perfection of mediumship or superiorness. It is about being gentle on yourself, patient with those you might work with (sitters, spirit communicators, working colleagues, and friends and family that are close to you, who may help you with your unfoldment), taking things at a realistic pace and putting aside all inhibiting goals and unhealthy beliefs that separate you from other people and life. The following are some of the things I have found helpful for achieving this, starting with the notion of trust I mentioned.

Trust

It is often said in Spiritualism that we must trust the spirit world; that we must trust our guides and helpers and trust what emanates beyond our normal reasoning and thinking capacities. While this may be true for us as we become more advanced in the unfolding of mediumship, this puts pressure on the beginner, on people who still have doubts and uncertainties as to whether or not spirit influences are true for them – even though they may be undergoing experiences that will eventually lead their awareness towards obvious spirit influences. Even so, their conscious mind may still be distrustful and doubtful, uncertain and questioning as to whether their experiences are real. It is only through constant exploration of any experiences that unfold and recognising those that point towards genuine spirit communication will a maturity of growth and trust in the spirit begin.

An authentic trust in the spirit is about embracing the beginning of a deep friendship between yourself and the invisible world of those that work with you. This trust is an evolving experience that builds over time and through the experiences you undergo. But the most important ingredient of trust, is trust in yourself and your abilities.

Sometimes sitters can tell you that the information you have given them about a spirit communicator is wrong. It is at such times that you might need to work harder with your mediumistic abilities in order to double check if the information is trustworthy evidence of survival, or whether you have misinterpreted something. It can be that the information you have given is not actually known by the sitters at that moment in time, but they may be able to check it later. You as the working medium might be able to receive further communication from the spirit world about who the sitters could ask or where the sitters would find confirmation about the information.

Is it real?

I have always found it helpful to look deeply into the validity of things I have experienced mediumistically, as well as reflect upon the things that others may teach as fact about mediumship. To establish an authentic understanding of mediumistic unfoldment, I believe it is important to arrive at a realisation of what is true for us, so that we embrace a sense of reality that can be both lived and expressed in our daily lives and work. Through this we come to realise that the world of the spirit, which is a part of our true self and all life, is intelligent, and that everything the spirit world communicates to and through us is based on this intelligence.

Through building the foundations of our beliefs on what has proved itself to be true, we avoid claims about spirit communication that are not grounded in truth. It is important to realise that it is through both intelligence and clear insights that we and the spirit world can blend together and bring to the world rational demonstrations of mediumship based on facts and evidence of survival after death.

Discernment

I have so far emphasised the importance of trust and reality. We also need to look closely at numerous levels of mind that exist, both incarnate and discarnate, and how they influence one another. We need to be aware of how all things affect us on a mental level and how our awareness affects communication with the discarnate world of the spirit. It is of course important to look at how our mind and beliefs affect communication with the spirit and how their influence and thoughts affect us. We need to do this in order to discover what is genuine awareness of the spirit and to discern how much our own minds may be influencing spirit communication.

In the beginning stages it can be difficult to distinguish between the two. We must therefore continue to work with our thoughts, our minds and spirit communicators seeking to work with us, to establish a breakthrough where we come to know the difference and start building authentic communications with those in the spirit world.

Sensitivity

We are all sensitive to internal and external worlds with which we come into contact, whether it be physically, psychologically or emotionally. The same holds true for mediums, no matter how well established they may be. To bring about wholesome growth, the sensitivity we have to all worlds of being (including the world of the spirit), requires us to become aware of our reactions and to recognise how all levels can affect us in different ways. It is through responsible engagement with our sensitive reactions that we make mature decisions about our life, our mediumistic abilities and the unfoldment of our spiritual nature. If we become spiritually engaged in understanding these sensitive areas that are parts of us and how they can lead us to being more whole and in harmony with life, we can then take on a willing and mature responsibility for our evolving sensitivity.

The spirit and our world

Sometimes I hear it said through different mediums in various states of trance or in public talks that the physical world in which we live is 'a dark and dismal place of suffering', as if this is imposed on us and is all there is to physical life – that only by becoming free from the physical realm will we be able to enter a world of light and beauty. If this were true, why is it that when we look at different auras surrounding human and other physical life, we see complexities of vibrant colours that are essential facets of the evolution and potential of all? There are of course, situations in human life that are less than perfect, and there is suffering in the world that has been inflicted upon others. There is also ignorance in the world and much that we can say about it that is negative. But this is only a partial reality and does not make physical life completely negative.

Photographs of Earth from outer space have shown that she is a beautiful blue and white sphere suspended in space. Earth has many natural places of great beauty that are breath-taking, which can lift our spirits in times of sadness. I personally feel we need to be careful of embracing ideas about the world as a totally dark place, as it can lead us to not caring enough about our relationships with other people and life. As far as I'm aware, spirit communicators that mediums work with have all had *physical lives* that still seem to influence their personality in some way.

There is great creativity in all: in Nature, art, parenthood, friendship, skilful social interaction, music, poetry, literature and so on. Positive changes have been made in the worlds of medicine, science and education. Great people have implemented ideas that have changed people's lives for the better.

It seems to me that even in various states of trance, some mediums are allowing themselves to be influenced by ideas that are interfering with the true message of the spirit. For I have only heard the spirit teach compassion and understanding, of which personal responsibility for how we think, feel and act is an indispensable ingredient.

Ultimately, as with all people following spiritual paths, mediums will need to consider how to unfold and develop a closer union with the Divine, with Nature and all of humankind. They will need to embrace ways in which to awaken within themselves a deeper creativity and appreciation of the awe inspiring evolving Universe in which we live. This includes awakening to the Earth's natural beauty and to realms of love and wisdom, as this will cultivate mediums' minds and characters.

All great teachers, such as Jesus, Krishna and the Buddha, taught about the importance of love for each other. Is it not time to embrace this? Any darkness will then give way to the light that shines within each of us and will help us connect with others in more natural and compassionate ways. Is this not the true message of the spirit and the deepest implications of a spiritual life?

Moving forward

Learning how to be still within, which does not imply inactivity, is crucial. But in stillness you will still have thoughts and reactions. As you become still, you will start to notice experiences to which you react (though perhaps the words *respond* or *engage with* might be better terms to use here). These reactions will over time, help you to understand different realities of experience and identify whether they have come from the spirit world or your own inner intuition, or past conditioning. There can also be times of uncertainty in unfoldment where things in our lives that we have suppressed or have been afraid to face may surface, which may leave us with a sense of concern. Endeavour if you can to work through such times of uncertainty. This is an important part of unfoldment, as it is about recognising who you truly are. Through this you will awaken to mediumistic experiences in their many forms which, if approached in the right way, will lead you to discover what awareness is truly about.

Proceed with an openness of mind and relax into the different dimensions of being that reveal themselves to you. Don't let fear enter your unfoldment, as there is ultimately nothing to be afraid of. The world of the spirit will join with you, and through this blending, you will find many wonderful and beautiful experiences that will enrich your life and the great work that lies ahead.

'Nothing is to be feared', as the saying goes, 'except fear itself'. So learn to recognise your fears, then let them go and share them with God and the spirit world. Seek their help and guidance, and from this, develop an attitude of fearlessness. Recognise in every situation how fear can affect you and hold you back. Don't deny it. Don't fight it. But accept it. This is the key to letting go. Acceptance is the key to everything because it means we are not fighting but embracing and accepting things that have happened. Therefore, we learn from experience and surrender all things that inhibit us, with a sense of understanding.

Openness

It is important for us to be receptive to the views of others and listen to them with an openness of mind and heart. This does not imply taking on everyone's ideas. If you meet someone who wishes to impose their beliefs, you must decide whether to allow it to happen. Linked with such things are agendas. Some people can be eager to impress others with their experiences, which can then cause others to measure their experiences against them and start to feel as though they are somehow lacking because things that have unfolded in their development do not match the other person's descriptions.

A word of caution needs to be made here. Don't allow this to happen or believe that there is anything to be gained by measuring your experiences with another's. On the one hand people can find comfort and reassurance in hearing about the paths others have taken and the variety of experiences that people have had. But there is obviously a difference between trying to *impress people with our experiences* and *simply sharing them*, as well as asking others about the things that have unfolded in their lives.

Ultimately it is about how mediumistic and spiritual experiences change us in positive and fruitful ways. If we are using them to make us seem more important, then we have unfortunately lost the reasons for encountering them. In truth, no one is better than anyone else. All are equal in the eyes of the spirit. All of us have equal opportunities to realise our true potential and live by it.

Stories

We often hear stories about ways people should approach development and mediumship, which can both illuminate and enlighten us. But there are also stories that have the opposite effect that we may have told ourselves or may have taken on board from others.

When we sit for the spirit, with the aim of exploring our mediumistic potential, we need to realise that we lose nothing by simply sitting and giving our time to the spirit, even if nothing appears to happen. If we look closely enough, we may find that our sitting has changed our attitudes to life in positive ways.

We may start sitting for development with set ideas about things we want and what we want to become, such as being a famous medium, a trance medium and so on. Such things can of course be barriers, as it may be that they are not right for us at a particular moment in time. This is why we need to look closely at our ongoing unfoldment and decide for ourselves whether something is helpful for our overall progress, irrespective of what we are told by others or have told ourselves. We must endeavour to enter development with open minds and not become prey to stories that inhibit our growth. You may become despondent at times, which can be perfectly natural. Growth invariably means going with and working through the highs as well as the lows of life.

I once heard a medium tell a group of students who had started to question whether to continue sitting in their development circle or not, that she knew a similar group who had decided not to sit as they believed they were not making any progress and at that point mediumistic physical phenomena started to happen.

The problem with such accounts is that it may have been the situation with the circle the medium mentioned, but it does not guarantee that the same will happen for the other group of students. There are many pitfalls and no clear answers. The story could even be seen to make the students who were thinking of giving up feel guilty, as though they didn't have enough faith and that was why they were failing. On the other hand it could have been there were problems with the overall dynamic of the group and it might have been better for them to disband and go their separate ways. It could even have been that they needed to change the way their circle was run – that they needed to unlearn and relearn how to approach their circle work. Ultimately only they would be able to decide the best way forward and what would be beneficial for all involved, including those who worked with them in the spirit world.

* * *

Exercise: three minute reflection

Be quiet for a few minutes and reflect upon the spirit within. Recognise that you are not separate from the spirit world, but are an intricate part of it. You are a spiritual being with infinite positive potential.

Sitting in
the Power

2

❖

The following exercise is called *Sitting in the Power*. It is a technique that I was given by the spirit world to use through the trance medium Mark Webb to teach and help people grasp the realities of what various powers and energies are about and ultimately to what we are all connected. It has proven to be one of the most popular exercises I use on my courses.*

To do this exercise you will need to sit and relax and as you do so, allow your whole body and mind to relax. Don't worry about results. The spirit world have told me that in using this practice, students will find themselves unfolding their natural mediumistic, psychic and spiritual abilities that are already there within them.

At the heart of this exercise is the realisation of our spiritual consciousness and its eternal relationship with the spirit world and the Divine. It promotes an awareness of our bodies, breath and patterns of thought and how they connect with the rhythms and energies of life, Nature and the Universe. The exercise also touches the powers that are within us, with our abilities to see, hear and feel. It also goes beyond these into realms of light and knowing and realising that this light is the dwelling place of the Divine. Here we allow ourselves to become in tune with Divine power, however we perceive it to be.

---

*Whenever Glyn led students through this exercise, he did it without a script and was each time inspired in the way he remembered the various stages and the detail of things he included.

This exercise is not about having to believe, but discovering for ourselves how the exercise can help us to change and help our natural mediumistic and psychic abilities to flourish. Time and time again I have found that what the spirit world have said about the abilities that can unfold through this exercise has been proven by those who have tried it for themselves. As the exercise has various sections to it, you may like to ask a friend to lead you through it or record yourself reading it and then meditate to your recording. Be sure to leave an appropriate length of space between the different sections if you do this.

1. Relax the body by consciously going slowly through the body, from the soles of the feet to the ankles, the lower legs, the knees, the upper legs, the hips, the buttocks, the lower and upper abdomen and back, the chest, the shoulders, the upper arms, the elbows, the lower arms, the wrists, the hands and fingers, the back and front of the neck, the jaw, the ears, the cheeks, the lips, the nose, the forehead and the back and top of the head. As you become aware of each area mentally/*silently* say to yourself, 'Relax' and let go of any tension with the out-breath.

2. Then become aware of these areas in the reverse order, starting with the top of the head down to the feet, consciously connecting with the Earth as you do this.

3. Be aware that you are now relaxed and know that your body possesses power. Then become aware of the rhythm

of your breath and as you breathe in, know that you are breathing in new life, new beginnings, opportunities and energy. As you breathe out, know that you are breathing out negativity and all that stands in your way. As you become aware of the rhythm of your breath, know that its rhythm is a rhythm of power.

4. As you relax and breathe in and out, know that you are sharing the power of life that is within and all around you and that there is no beginning or end to this continuous interaction. As you do this, notice the power that is there flowing through physical existence. Continue this for a short while.

5. On the in- and out-breath feel yourself starting to expand, rather like blowing yourself up as a balloon. With each in- and out-breath notice yourself expanding further and become used to this feeling. Realise that this expanded awareness is your own spirit Self expanding. Acknowledge that this expansion is not limited by time and space and can expand eternally with the natural rhythms of life. As you expand in this way, notice that you are beginning to go beyond the body and the place in which you are sitting.

6. Within your awareness of your breath, your spirit and this expanded state, become aware of standing on the Earth, on Gaia, and as you breathe in and out, notice how your spirit connects with and expands naturally into the whole of the Earth. Notice how you are able to touch the power of the

Earth. As you breathe in and out, expand more and more, both into and around the Earth.

Within this awareness, realise that your spirit is able to connect with and penetrate all living forms of existence, including the mineral, sea, animal, bird, plant and tree kingdoms and queendoms – the whole of Nature – and is able to touch all the power and light that exists within these living and evolving things. Naturally flow with the powers of Nature, with the flowing of the rivers, with the air, with human life, and with the smallest and largest of activities that are parts of Nature and the natural rhythms of life. Expand more and more into these things. Touch and realise the connections you share with the power of all life, consciousness and creation that is in all life and the living Earth.

Expand as a spirit and touch this oneness with the in- and out-breath. This is not a wish, but a deep knowing and blending with the power and unity of all. Stay and relax with this knowing for a while.

7. As you breathe in and out, realise that you are going beyond the interconnected realms of Earth, Nature and human existence. Notice your awareness flowing through and how it is connected to each planet, star and galaxy and the vastness of space and the Universe. Notice that the physical substance of which you are now aware has within it an essence of the spirit. Recognise that the creative powers of life that are within the Universe are also parts of you. Stay with your awareness of these things for a while.

8. With each in- and out-breath, know that your spirit is taking you to the many powers and energies of the world of thought, which have no end – thought that is present, past and connected with the future.

9. Relax on the out-breath and as you breathe in and out become aware of your consciousness expanding to the many levels and layers of mental mediumship. As you breathe in and out, touch the energy of mental mediumship that is already within you. This is not about contact with others in the spirit world but touching the power and energy that is there within your own spirit, knowing that the potential for all that you can become and unfold is there within you. Stay with this awareness for a while.

10. Relax on the out-breath and as you breathe in and out become aware that within you is a light that grows brighter with every round of breath. Become this light with each breath. As you become this light, notice within it is an ultimate power. Realise that within you, God dwells, how Divine power has sparked off something within you, how it has lit your inner being with a radiance and a light. As you breathe in and out and expand as a spirit, as pure consciousness, as a force of creativity, notice this light becoming brighter and brighter and that you are starting to shine. Recognise that you are a living light, and how this light permeates the whole of your spirit and connects with all power, including spiritual and creative energies. Stay with this for a while.

11. As you breathe in and out and awaken to the light within you, become aware of a brighter and greater light surrounding and joining you. It is a light that connects both within and beyond you and beyond all things. It is a spiritual realm that connects with infinity and eternity. As it surrounds your spirit and your inner light, you become brighter and more radiant. Begin to realise that you are in God's dwelling place.

In time as you practice this exercise, this place that connects with and is also beyond all places, will become more real and known to you. Here you awaken to and acknowledge the reality of all power, thought and life that exists, is known and understood. This is where the individual consciousness of your spirit will come to understand the essential vibration of life – a power that is in every thing, thought, breath, spirit and life and its manifestation (animate and inanimate). Here you are able to blend with realms of infinity. For you have within you infinite potential. You have God-like qualities within you. Stay with this awareness for a while.

12. Be still and let the energies and vibrations you have become aware of in this exercise flow through you and your consciousness. Within time you will come to know what is real and unreal, what is true and what is false. Just allow yourself to be open to this knowing for a while. If your mind becomes distracted, do not worry. Just become aware of it drifting, then gently bring your awareness back to the exercise and the awareness it has awakened within you.

13. Now become aware of the place you are sitting and the weight of your body on the ground, cushion or chair you are sitting on. With each in- and out-breath, return to your physical state, bringing with you all that you have discovered within you. Realise you have established levels of power and knowing that you can take with you into your daily life and that the more you become aware of these things, they will grow and encourage more expanded states that connect with the spirit that you are and the spirit world that is both within and around you at all times.

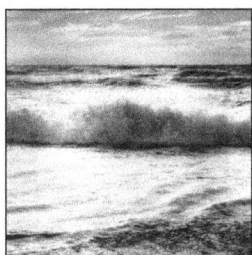

Psychic & Mediumistic
Unfoldment

3

❖

I once gave a series of three sittings to a couple who had never been involved in mediumship or Spiritualism before. They had lost their 19 year old daughter, who was their only child. I found this young woman in the spirit to be one of the most objective communicators I had ever worked with. She was joyful, enthusiastic and delighted that she could communicate through me to her parents with both ease and precision.

The parents were equally delighted with the evidence and communication that the daughter was able to give. As the medium, I was obviously pleased with the daughter's ability to communicate so naturally. It was for me as though we had known each other all our lives. The communication between us felt so alive. She gave facts about her personality, understanding of life and how for no known reason as far as medical science could ascertain, her heart had stopped and she passed to the spirit world.

After the second sitting, the daughter asked if the parents would be willing to see a medium who was also a psychic artist, who was coming to the area in a few weeks' time. The daughter asked me to promise not to say anything about her communication with me to the visiting psychic artist. I obviously made this promise.

The parents booked a sitting with the medium under assumed names and went to see her. As their sitting began, the medium started to draw and spoke about having a young girl present and said that she was about 18 or 19 years old and that she had promised through another medium to endeavour to come and be drawn at this sitting. The parents informed the medium that this was correct.

As the medium began to draw and the drawing started to take shape, it started to show more and more of the exact likeness of the daughter. During this sitting the daughter mentioned various things that I had also given as evidence to the parents such as how she had died, that she was at university at the time and so on. Interestingly I had previously given the parents the daughter's Christian name, whereas the psychic artist gave her second name. Yet in the last sitting I gave the parents, the daughter repeated her second name several times, which I had not known before.

For the parents, the sittings that both the psychic artist and I had given them, amounted to what they described as 'incontrovertible evidence'. For them, they both felt and knew beyond doubt that their daughter had survived death and that they would meet her again in another life.

This series of sittings I gave the parents showed me that those in the spirit world are both enthusiastic and happy to prove their survival to those they love. As mediums we are merely their mouth piece. Mediumship itself is about learning to become the instrument through which spirit personalities such as the sitters' daughter are able to communicate.

Facets of spirit communication

Psychic and mediumistic powers have manifested in many of the inspiring spiritual traditions of both the East and West. They have been experienced in numerous mystical and spiritual states of awareness and are common to many people. Powers that we call psychic have no boundaries, whether they manifest mediumistically, artistically or as pure intuition. They exist in an infinite variety of forms and can possess great value in the different ways they manifest.

The intuitive self, the knower that knows the unknown, the shaman that sees into the vision quest, the yogi that develops the *siddhis* (miraculous powers), the seer that sees into the possible, the sensitive who has the ability to communicate with many levels of life and with those that we love, will all come to discover that there are no limitations to the various powers they possess. They are all facets of our true spirit Self.

The spiritual and the psychic

Much has been written about psychic and mediumistic phenomena. Some writers believe that psychic and mediumistic abilities are detrimental to various areas of spiritual life. But this is only true if they are developed at the expense of spiritual awareness and practices of compassion, kindness, inclusiveness, unity, discernment and other attributes of a spiritual life and consciousness.

Others believe that mediumship is a spiritual gift, separate from the psychic aspect of our nature. Some teachers of mediumship tell us that it is higher than psychic realms of knowledge – an altogether finer vibration that is separate from psychic abilities.

Yet if we look closely at mediumship, it becomes clear that it is a facet of our psychic being and is *not necessarily* a spiritual power if used in isolation from other areas of unfoldment. Like any other abilities we have, the responsibility of making mediumistic paths spiritual forces for good is down to us as individuals. In reality, mediumship works through the same internal mechanisms of perception that we use to perceive regular physical life.

From one perspective, we see that the unfoldment of mediumship *by itself* does not require us to awaken to recognised qualities of spirituality. To become in tune with spiritual realms of life and action needs individual commitment and a deeper understanding of the Divinity of all.

These points are made not to discredit the views of others, but to emphasize that our spiritual growth is in our own hands. Even though any effort we are prepared to make spiritually will attract corresponding influences that will enhance our unfoldment, it is still up to us to take the first step.

Levels of awareness

There is much that we still do not understand about the human mind and how to awaken to different realms of our spiritual nature. In the past we may have been influenced in our thinking by the beliefs of others. Now we must take the opportunity to discover for ourselves their truth or falsehood.

There are problems in trying to distinguish too sharply between inspirational and intuitive knowledge, the psychic, the mediumistic and the spiritual, the prophet and the activist, the mystic and the seer, as there is no clear point where one of them ends and another begins. All have their origins in our being and are expressions of an interactive whole, which consists of our spirit, mind, feelings and body. All are but a flowing towards a discovery of the infinite potential in all.

These powers that manifest in our unfoldment are simply a means by which we can demonstrate that there is something beyond materialistic realms of experience.

*   *   *

Exercises: psychic and mediumistic experiments
In each of the following two experiments, start by placing yourself in a calm and relaxed frame of mind. Try to be as descriptive as possible. Afterwards analyse all the information that came to you and determine how subjective or objective the information was.

Bear in mind that impressions or images of a symbolic nature may come, which you will have to probe in order to discover their true meaning. At first it may not be obvious that an impression or image is symbolic. The following observation by Santoshan illustrates this:

I once subjectively saw a monk, which at first seemed to represent a spirit communicator or guide. It was only after analysing this image and seeing how it looked more like a caricature than a real person that I realised it was a way of telling me that someone was connected with the surname of 'Monk'. On the same occasion I was shown lipstick being applied. This was a way of conveying the surname of 'Yardley'.*

Check any impression or information received for its validity and consider how best to transmit it to those that would be the recipients of it. It is important to ask questions like, 'Why am I being shown this?' and 'What does it mean?' If you are not prepared to do this, you may miss some important and evidential information, and what you give as evidence may be incorrect. So remember that there may be times when what you perceive appears to be wrong, but what may actually be incorrect is your interpretation.

Experiment 1

1. Ask a friend who you do not know so much about (perhaps someone who has only recently become a friend) to sit in a chair opposite you.

2. Put aside all that you know about your friend. Try to sense that friend physically. Find out information about his or her physical life without asking any questions.

---

*Glyn especially asked for this paragraph to be included in this chapter.

This could be related to your friend's character or work, or to the people with whom he or she works. Find out any information that could be used to prove that you are obtaining these details through your psychic senses.

Experiment 2

This is a basic exercise in which persistence will prove beneficial. Remember that mistakes are as helpful as accuracy.

1. In this experiment, try to obtain some information from the spirit world that links with your friend that proves survival after death of the physical body. When seeking this communication, be aware if you are seeing clairvoyantly. If so, describe whether you are seeing subjectively or objectively (either seeing in your mind's eye or as though the communicator is a physical person in front of you).

2. Try to be aware of the communicator speaking to you. Notice how you are sensing. If you receive any information, pass it on to your friend. By doing this, you are bringing your friend into contact with all that is happening to you and encouraging him or her to be an active participant.

Note: As I have asked you to choose a friend in this experiment, it will be helpful to place all opinion and knowledge of him or her aside. You will find that doing this will help you to depend more on your psychic senses and the spirit world's influence.

Exercises: sensing the aura

The following exercises will increase your sensitivity to energies in the human aura.

Exercise 1

To begin to sense the aura, place both hands together in an attitude of prayer. Draw your hands out to the level of your shoulders. Keep your eyes open and your awareness centred in the space between the palms. Slowly bring them nearer until you feel that you have an invisible balloon between your palms. This is the energy from your physical aura.

Exercise 2

Stand one pace back behind a friend, holding your hands up (palms facing forwards) and move slowly towards your friend until you can sense his or her aura, approximately two inches away from his or her shoulders. Try to sense the energy of your friend's aura in your hands.

Ask your friend to recall different memories such as those associated with joy and happiness, fear or hate, or thoughts of someone they love or loved who is either living on Earth or in the spirit world. Ask your friend to think of healing and to imagine various colours. See if you can sense a change in the energies around him or her and check with your friend the changes you felt.

Suggestions for further exercises

(a) If you are an objective clairvoyant (the ability to see spirit personalities in an almost physical way instead of a mental impression), look at people and see if you can begin to perceive a kind of misty outline around them. Keep this in clairvoyant view and see what may build from this. If you see colour, be aware that it emanates from the person. Try to understand what it tells you about him or her.

(b) Take a flower. Go beyond its physical shape with the mind and find out what you see and feel. Try to understand its energy.

(c) Hold an object that belongs to someone and use psychometry (the ability to feel an object psychically and pick up information relating to the person that it belongs) to sense the aura and see what information comes from it.

Psychometry is a useful tool as it relates to the aura and enables you to understand a person's psychic activity. It is one of the most useful abilities a medium can develop.

On another level psychometry can be used to link with the actual physical origins of an object, instead of people associated with it, such as information about the part of the world it came from, or what materials have made it.

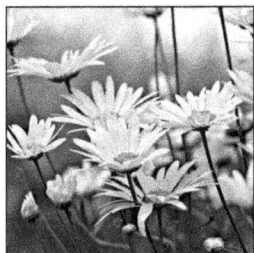

The Mediumistic Journey

_____

4

❖

I remember arriving to take the Sunday service at the old Longton Spiritualist Church. Because I had arrived a little early, the medium Gordon Higginson, who was the president of the church, was the only person there to greet me. As usual at Longton Church I went into the mediums' lounge to wait until I was needed for the service and the evening demonstration of mediumship.

Some minutes later Gordon entered the room with a pot of freshly brewed tea. After laying the tea pot down on a coffee table he suddenly turned to me and asked what was wrong with me and said,

Every time you sit you're wanting this or hoping that something might happen. All the time you're seeking for improvement during your sitting. Your mind is full of this. But it is proving to be a barrier to the spirit world. Just sit' and allow the spirit to work with you and use you. Instead of presenting them with all your wants, start discovering why they have come, what they are seeking to unfold within and through you and this way you will acquire the power to become a more responsive medium that communicates more naturally with the spirit world.

The lesson I learned through this short conversation with a greatly loved friend and colleague was quite simple and applies to all who are embarking on mediumistic journeys. It is about being open and responsive to the spirit and learning not to impose our personal wants, needs and demands. Of course, continuous growth is important, but there are also times when we need to let go and simply blend with the spirit.

Ultimately in the unfoldment of mediumship there are no set rules to follow to reach a specific goal. There are only guidelines and pointers that can be offered. Each of us will have to decide which roads we wish to take that are best suited to our nature. When approached in a healthy way, we discover that mediumistic unfoldment is an active and evolving path that leads to new and profound experience and deep contact with the world of the spirit.

The eternal spirit

Part of our unfoldment involves realising that our true nature has never been born and never dies; it is eternal and full of infinite potential. Through mediumistic powers we come to know this truth for ourselves.

The worldwide interest we see happening into realms of psi-phenomena, prophecy, seership, mediumship and spirituality shows a growing thirst for something more than everyday material existence. All these realms are filled with creative potential, transforming wisdom and infinite possibilities.

These are not worlds of entertainment or about escapism but are facets of being that can be life affirming and life transforming. They are about discoveries of inner powers that open us to our true purpose and a profound understanding of life's deepest mysteries. They show and teach us that we are more than just our bodies – that our individual being and consciousness have no limitations and are facets of a spiritual source.

Our bodies exist because of their spiritual counterpart. The spirit seeks to express itself through our bodies, minds and feelings in order to influence all that we do. There is no end to our evolvement and the potential within us. It is only we who limit ourselves with inhibiting beliefs about our inherent gifts.

When we focus on and work with our inner abilities, we unfold mediumistic powers and the vision of the seer and the prophet. Nothing then remains hidden or unknown. We allow our growth to unfold naturally and become aware of our own authentic spirit and the many levels of Divinity and creativity that exist, including after death states and the ability to commune with helpers who connect with numerous spheres of existence.

When we awaken to these different worlds, we come to realise the interconnectedness of all, how all things exist in the Divine and the spirit and how they are profoundly interwoven. We realise that life is eternal and never dies. Such things lead us to a discovery of our greatest qualities of love, compassion, kindness and unity with all.

A kaleidoscope of possibilities

Mediumship is about allowing beneficial transformations to happen and embodying them within us. In its ultimate sense it is about manifesting a genuine concern and willingness to be of service to others, irrespective of obstacles and rewards we may encounter.

At its finest, mediumistic unfoldment is about embracing actions that bring about positive changes. To think of the spirit world as purely transcendent and overlook the immanent, omnipresent and creative aspects of its sacredness means overlooking essential areas of potential. If we allow it, the mediumistic journey becomes multifaceted and opens us to infinite possibilities of growth. This does not set us apart from everyday existence. If approached from a spiritual perspective, mediumistic abilities help us to engage more healthily with life.

Those who are open and inclusive in the paths they tread, will find more areas of their lives receptive to unfoldment and will take part in the spirit's work in more fruitful ways. The time to start out on this quest is now, as the present holds many possibilities. All we need to do is be responsive to positive growth and willing to be more active instruments for the compassionate and creative work of the spirit.

The mediumistic gift

For me, mediumistic abilities have not only given me an opportunity to communicate with those who have continued their existence after death of the physical body, but also to view the cause of all phenomena – to realise that there is that which transcends all and is the originator, the preserver and the creator of all. If we lose sight of this I feel we will be in danger of losing sight of the deeper dimensions of spirituality and mediumship and any abilities we have will suffer, as we will only be going so far with them and placing limitations upon them. If we take a more holistic approach, we are not in any danger of limiting the emergence of our spiritual evolution and any abilities we have. A balanced combination of the spirit, the intuitive, mental, emotional and physical levels of our being will produce a balanced, well-rounded approach to life and unfoldment.

Our mediumistic legacy

Through mediumistic experience we discover knowledge of another life from which we came and to which we will return. There has always existed in humankind's psyche the belief in nonphysical realms of existence. Throughout the ages ancestor worship has been intrinsically bound-up with many traditions.

In all the great spiritual traditions contact with other realms has been mentioned and has throughout history to the present day been practised. There have even been accounts of angelic beings communicating with various people. There are also shamans and oracles who are consulted in various traditions and many renowned mystics have displayed mediumistic abilities.

Early indigenous people and shamans were the first to connect with a spirit world permeating Nature and to communicate with their departed ancestors. Others have looked for more transcendent worlds of spirituality. Although there are some who have never completely separated themselves from early indigenous beliefs and practices, there are some who have, which has led to an unhealthy separation between Nature and the spirit. All areas need to be included in the search for the one ultimate spiritual reality that expresses itself in and through all.

If we accept that life is eternal and there are other realms of existence intertwined with our physical world, then it must be a natural step in our evolution to be able to communicate with these other realms and with those who are living on. We need to recognise that there are different ways in which to approach the many faceted dimensions of spirituality and mediumship and of being open to areas that can lead us to healthier states of spiritual being and embracing the all-ness of what eternal life is about.

The phenomena of mediumship

There is a tremendous amount of data that is now available to us about people who have undertaken certain practices, such as prayer, meditation and mantra, within their own faith and spiritual traditions, who have experienced other levels of reality and realms of spirit communication. Through such practices phenomena have manifested of both a mental and physical kind.

It is not just through what some may term as 'mediumistic practices' that such things have occurred. An illustration of what I mean by this can be seen in the fields of yoga where students have experienced spontaneous awakenings to clairvoyant, clairaudient and clairsentient abilities that were totally unsought and came about because of the practices they were doing.

Because mediumship has to work through our finite physical mind, our prevalent state of awareness and the beliefs we hold will condition its manifestation. This is one reason why we need to include other practices such as spiritual principles and understanding as they help us to transcend limiting concepts, beliefs and finite thoughts, and open us more to the infinite mind that is present in all.

An unfoldment to all possibilities

I believe we are born with a predisposition for mediumistic abilities. From my experience, these abilities take us into realms of potential and individual possibilities. It is through recognition, receptivity, opening our minds and working with our potential that an awareness of there being no limit to the inherent abilities we have comes into being.

Psychic and mediumistic powers in this sense are neither given nor developed but are *revealed* when we remove all that stops us from recognising them as integral parts of our nature. Unfoldment in these areas then lies in how we reach this level of understanding and manifest these powers more purely. Ideas some have about mediums being *born* rather than *made* are misleading, as everyone has the potential for mediumistic abilities.

Readers will notice that I often use the term 'unfoldment' when writing about how we can attune to various states and establish various stages. This is because no matter what potential abilities we have, we will still need to awaken to, unfold and learn how best to be aware of them and understand how to engage healthily with our ongoing growth.

We will notice as time progresses and we open up to our potential that the call of the spirit – the spirit's influence interacting with our everyday thoughts and actions – will deepen and change. Because of this, it is important not to be inflexible or narrow in our outlook, but open to all possibilities. As we develop a deeper response to and an understanding of our sensitivity and spiritual and psychic nature, we allow the spirit's presence to manifest more fully in our lives and guide us onto richer planes of being and consciousness.

By remaining open to all possibilities, we find ourselves unfolding a variety of previously hidden potentials and awakening to greater knowledge and insight. We will find that the more open our minds are, the more receptive we will be to mediumistic abilities and numerous spiritual gifts.

Becoming aware of the spirit

To sit in stillness and quietness and invite the spirit world to work with and through us is important, as our invitation shows a willingness to co-operate with the spirit and what may unfold through this. Through inviting the spirit to blend with our consciousness and to make themselves known through our senses, mediumistic abilities can be brought into being. At first there needs to be this intention of being willing to co-operate, eventually followed by letting this intention and willingness go, allowing our thoughts to become calmer and more settled and adopting an attitude of receptivity to different realms of being.

I think it is important that developing mediums come to truly know who is working with them in the spirit world. By knowing I do not mean by just name or nationality but learning through the communication that is established, the personality and identity of those working with them and begin to recognise how the unfoldment of mediumistic abilities influences them and how communication shapes itself through their individual awareness.

I think it is essential to realise that the two levels of communication that exist within mediumship are an evolving experience between the medium who is learning how best to apprehend information coming from the spirit world and this other level of reality learning how best to transmit information to the medium.

*   *   *

Exercise: developing your powers of description

In the demonstration of clairvoyance, clairaudience and clairsentience, the clarity of description plays an integral part. It is therefore important to develop the ability to interpret clearly and describe accurately what you see, hear or feel, as this will help to develop the quality of your mediumship.

Although the following exercises may appear to have nothing to do with psychic or mediumistic abilities, they will in fact help you to develop the ability to describe things more accurately. The exercises are designed to help you to use natural means of description to convey specific information. You will find that this will be of great value when it comes to conveying any mediumistic evidence.

1. Ask a friend to sit with you and then describe to him or her someone who is known to you both but without saying his or her name. Try to describe this person's character, personality, sex, age, height, hair, build, manner, dress, distinguishing features etc. See if your friend can recognise the person you are describing.

2. Describe details of a place, without naming the area that is known to you and your friend. Outline its main features. For example, whether it is an area of a city or countryside. Describe any buildings, road layout and so on, and see if your friend can recognise the place.

3. Describe to your friend, without naming them, various types of objects in common everyday use, especially ones known to you both that may be associated with people you know. Do not name the objects and see if your friend can identify them from your descriptions.

Developing Mediumistic Powers

5

❖

To my understanding, all of us are born with the potential of mediumistic awareness and, of course, spiritual knowledge – that every spirit that incarnates in the human realm brings with it a variety of mediumistic abilities and wholesome qualities.

We only have to look at the array of experience and abilities that manifest within us as individuals (which come about because of the creativity of the spirit in all) to see that we are more than just physical beings. Even when we talk to another person in the physical world we are in fact communicating with another spirit personality, because of the spirit that exists in all people, species and things.

If we wish to discover our inherent mediumistic potential, we will have to explore individually various powers and realms of the spirit and how they relate to and can affect us. Advice and encouragement we may receive from other people can also be of great help, but we will also have to believe in ourselves and our own inner experiences and discerning intuition.

What can often seem like wrong turns, false starts or mistakes might discourage us. But invariably these things help us to refine our awareness and lead us to firmer convictions about the paths we must tread.

When we look at people developing mediumistic abilities, we often find them making statements such as, 'I think I saw, felt or heard something'. Instead we need to contemplate whether or not we are *really* feeling, seeing or hearing something of a mediumistic nature and learn how to distinguish the difference between imagination and the spirit working through and with our mind, thoughts and senses. This way developing mediums will begin to look constructively at their abilities. They will then begin to recognise the difference between individual imagination, doubt, receptivity and certainty. It is often just a lack of self-trust that holds people back.

An instrument for the activity of spirit

In the development of mediumship the same laws and power manifest through us all. We need to be conscious of how mediumistic gifts work through us and how they will be affected by our personality and character. Our individual unfoldment is affected by how we and the spirit work upon the potential within us. It is also affected by our aspirations and willingness to co-operate with the spirit world and by the spirit's ability to influence us at various levels of our being.

Some people have tried to standardise methods of development. This has been partly due to them believing that because their method was right for them, it must be right for everyone. But because of our individuality, this is not so. We must never impose our ideas on others, or insist that others follow the exact pattern of development we have taken, as this can only be harmful psychologically and spiritually. It is God and the spirit working through our individuality, character and personality that needs to be the ground on which our unfoldment begins.

Endeavour to link with God and the spirit influences that surround you and gain guidance and direction from them. Look at ways to encourage others and yourself to be open, straightforward, discerning and perform compassionate actions whenever you can. Through this, the influence of God and spirit will establish itself so that they and you will be of greater service to humanity and life on Earth.

Guidelines for successful circle work

Though some mediums have developed their mediumistic abilities by sitting alone or with only one other person, many mediums choose to develop their gifts in a development circle made up of three or more people. The following are some pointers to consider for successful mediumistic circle work.

1. Sitters in a mediumistic development circle

The sitters need to be sincere, well-balanced people whose minds are open and hopefully of a spiritual temperament, whose main aim is to build a link of communication with the spirit world. The purpose of a development circle is for its members to progress to a point at which they open to the spirit's influence and through that discover various truths about the spirit. Crucially there needs to be an aspiration to move towards spiritual realms of perception.

2. Time and place for a mediumistic development circle

Sitting at a regular time and place is important because it brings discipline into your life and the development of the circle. As time goes on and somebody shows signs of mediumship, you will realise that this has helped to establish the right atmosphere and vibration. This will enable the circle to jointly assist in the unfoldment of various levels of mediumship.

3. Potential

Sitters may show signs of mediumistic potential. If you are unsure about your abilities, do not be deterred from sitting and exploring possibilities of potential.

4. Attitude

Respectfulness and the desire to be of use to the spirit world are essential, as is a willingness to dedicate time to explore and understand dimensions relating to the spirit world and its implications.

5. Co-operation and experiences

All sitters will need to learn how to co-operate with each other and the spirit world, as well as how to interpret any experiences they have whilst sitting. Keep a level head and do not attach ideas to anything that might happen until it is proven beyond reasonable doubt.

The development circle's motive

The best advice for anyone starting a mediumistic development circle is to have plenty of patience. Be prepared to sit regularly over a period of time and let the presence of the spirit build. Do not try to force the circle's progress.

This is why it is important to choose your group of sitters carefully in order to have no friction, physically, mentally or emotionally. You need to have a common aim, interest and dedication.

An important aspect of successful circle work is the motive of the sitters. Ask yourself what your motive is behind your desire to sit and develop. It would not be advisable to sit if all you want to do is play around with psychic powers, as this is not enough for the spirit. Ultimately your motive needs to be about selfless service. If it is, you will find you will unfold greater gifts and qualities. The spirit seeks to help you discover your spiritual powers, which are and always have been inherent within you.

Some suggestions for practical do's and don'ts

1. Do take note of any feelings, experiences or occurrences while sitting. For example, spinning, floating, facial or cobweb sensations, light bands around the head, bodily heaviness, changes in the rhythm of breathing, the desire to stand, the desire to speak, seeing pinpricks or flashes of light, or the feeling of presences – the impression of a person, whether they are male or female, tall or short, strong or frail etc.

2. Do not interfere, but allow events to occur naturally. You do not know at this stage whether a sensation is due to a spirit personality, to the body relaxing, or to the effect of a change in your breathing pattern. Your aim simply needs to be about exploring possibilities and what might

be happening.

3. Do enjoy, in a relaxed way, all that happens, even if it is just a feeling of being relaxed in the body and mind and a sense of well-being.

4. Do not be nervous about anything that happens. Nothing can or will harm you. Just continue to be calm, relaxed and at peace.

5. Do remember that the spirit are trying to make themselves known through your psychic and mediumistic senses. Understand that the spirit have to work through your mind and consciousness, so their task is difficult. Therefore accept that the circle may take time to develop.

6. Do not be quick to judge any experience as being genuine or imaginary, or any impression as being your guide or a specific person, until you are sure beyond reasonable doubt that it is so. This point is of great importance as psychic and mediumistic sensitivity can make people impressionable, so keep a level head at all times.

7. Do remember that you will go through some peculiar experiences. The more familiar you become with them, the greater your understanding, responsiveness and sensitivity will be. You will also expand the range of your unfoldment.

Sitting for the potential trance medium

We now come to the role that circle sitters play in the development of trance mediumship. Regularity and punctuality are essential. All sitters are required first of all to be level-headed and not inclined to jump to conclusions. They must be able to distinguish fact from fantasy and willing to devote their time and energy to the development of a potential trance medium. The sitters should not try to accomplish this by means of force, but by patience and accepting that the spirit may creatively draw upon energies they need to quicken the development of the medium in the direction they wish his or her unfoldment to go.

The sitters may observe certain changes occurring to the medium, which can indicate the development of entrancement. The medium may suddenly jerk slightly or experience vibratory, trembling sensations and report temporary loss of physical awareness. The medium might afterwards describe prickling on the skin's surface like mild static shocks or a feeling of wanting to stand and speak.

Everything that happens should be accepted calmly and rationally, with no time limit, presupposition or restriction placed upon what is happening or when it will be developed. At all times the medium needs to be encouraged to carry on working until the stage comes when the spirit proves itself. When it does, the spirit may be asked for further direction and guidance for the circle.

With the unfoldment of trance, as with all mediumistic abilities, perseverance is essential. In the initial stages there is often very little to show for the efforts put in by individual members of the circle. Nonetheless, dedication will bring rewards.

Remember that this is an experiment by you and the spirit world and that both sides of life are endeavouring to co-operate. Therefore, you need not be discouraged by what may appear to be failure or by any long periods of inactivity, as you never know what your efforts have achieved and what changes you have brought about.

Sitting for the potential physical medium

If someone is already showing obvious signs of physical mediumship, the lead may be taken from this, i.e. sit for that person to see what may develop. When it is not known whether anyone has such potential, it is best to sit in a normal manner with the intention that the spirit world will guide and eventually direct you to sit for one particular circle member.

The reason you will be asked to sit for this person is that all the energies – psychic, physical and mental – from you and the medium may be utilised for the development of physical mediumship. The spirit world will use these energies to experiment with the sensitivity of the medium and with the environment of the physical circle.

Final points to consider

Approach circle work as an act of dedication and selfless service to the spirit world and of creatively assisting in the unfoldment of spiritual wisdom and proof of survival after death. Do not let discordant thoughts or disappointments affect the finer vibrations of the spirit, as these can have an adverse effect upon a medium's progress.

It is for this reason that a harmony of thought and attitude in all aspects of unfoldment ought to be included as a part of the circle's development. Without it, successful development will be hard to achieve.

The Spirituality
of Mediumship

6

❖

The following list can be looked upon as the spiritual implications of mediumship.

1. Proof of survival

In its deepest sense, proof of survival awakens a realisation of the implications of our eternal existence. It is not about focusing on where we will go at a later stage in our life but about the here and now and how we act and can grow in our daily interactions with others – with other people and species – and our everyday awareness of the spirit world. From proof of survival we come to realise that we have never been born and will never die.

All physical life on our planet has been given birth by Mother Earth. And within physical life there is the essence of spirit that has always existed. It is the animating force of all life. It has imbued our physical bodies with life, breath, consciousness, awareness and love.

We may have been educated to only understand the physical world, but the implications of survival encourage us to look deeper into life – to consider after death states, the interactive relationships we have with Nature and our relationships with God and the spirit world. When we examine these areas it becomes apparent that there is a force, an energy and a power that pervades all life, creation and the Universe. Through this we begin to understand that all forms of life are sacred, that Mother Earth herself is sacred. We come to realise that everything survives and that embedded within the Universe is creativity itself. And when we create in wholesome ways, we take an active role in the creativity of the Universe, God and the spirit world.

2. Sisterhood and brotherhood and the sacredness of human and non-human life

The first point then leads on to this second one, which encourages us to understand that not only does the same spirit exist in all, but that it is also individualised. As we investigate this, we begin to recognise that we are facets of Divinity in individualised form, and it is because of this that we possess the power to create. An integral part of this mystery is the recognition of our sisterhood and brotherhood with all people and species. This encourages us to revere the Divinity and same spirit in all. As we do this, respect and the ability to love all equally becomes a crucial facet of our lives.

3. The evolving spirit

Here we are faced with situations that can be based upon beliefs and personal experiences of the spirit's evolvement.

We are told by spirit communicators that progression is open to us all. This not only implies progression of our thoughts and actions here but also after death. This implies that the world of choice (choosing to evolve in our spiritual growth) is a part of natural progression. It is not about blindly following what the spirit world or mediums tell us we should do, but a personal discovery of what is true for us and our individual responsibility to grow and become wiser.

When we travel along this path, we notice that our growth leads us to qualities of compassion and understanding and the light that is within us all. Such qualities, along with this illuminating light, have the power to transform us into enlightened beings in the here and now of physical life as well as in our eternal spirit life.

4. Communicating with the spirit

We will notice in authentic communication that the spirit world will not impose their ideas. Spirit communication seeks to prove to humanity that all life survives death. It seeks to encourage us to reflect upon life, upon our beliefs and actions and be personally responsible for the evolution of our spiritual nature.

Those that work with us in the spirit world are there to guide and inspire us. From them comes love, understanding and encouragement. For they live in a world where nothing is criticized or condemned. This does not mean that they have lost their opinions or have sacrificed their natural intelligence. They themselves have chosen to come back and work with us in order that their love and concerns for us and their encouragement may open our perceptions and awareness of their world – to know that from spirit we have come and to spirit we will return, that our true natures are imbued with compassion, kindness, friendship and love.

When we link with those in the spirit world and to what they are seeking to encourage, we discover that their central message is about loving one another, understanding one another, helping one another, inspiring one another, being compassionate to each other and respectful of each other and life. It is through this that the deepest levels of communication with the spirit can be reached, expressed and established. So here we are once again encouraged to look at the responsibility we have toward our unfoldment and our mediumship and how to express it compassionately in everyday life.

5. Divine life

We are all individually responsible for what we believe. Beliefs that are grounded in reality come through personal investigation. The work of the spirit does not ask us to blindly accept anything. Our paths can lead us through many changes and sometimes U-turns, but this is all a part of individual discovery and learning. As mentioned, the spirit world constantly seeks to encourage us in our quests to be open to the varieties of experience we encounter and to investigate what they mean and imply.

Linking in with the unfoldment of mediumistic abilities is a recognition of a God of love – a God that is benevolent. This is my belief, which has come about through my own investigation and numerous experiences I have had. But you must decide for yourself.

It was interesting to talk to the editor of this compilation, Santoshan, and speaking to him about his experience as a Religious Studies school teacher. He mentioned that one of the first things he would ask the youngest pupils was what his role as an RS teacher implied. 'Was it about telling them what to think?' 'No', they would reply, 'That's not your job. You are here to tell us about different beliefs and ideas, but not what we are meant to believe'. I find it encouraging that children as young as 11 years old can be so wise. They knew intuitively that spirituality and beliefs were in their own hands. This does not mean they should not listen to different points of view and reflect upon them. Nonetheless, it ultimately implies making up their own minds about what they wish to believe, based on knowledge, insight and experience.

Spirituality doesn't demand that we become God-conscious. Goodness, God-consciousness, compassion, understanding, love and wisdom may be the qualities and ground of our true nature, but it is we who have to decide how open we can be to manifesting these things in our lives. Goodness itself doesn't require a belief in God for it to manifest as a natural part of our being.

For many, goodness comes from the spirit and is seen as a universal energy and eternal intelligence that they call 'God'. So investigate and allow yourself to find out what these things mean to you and whether they have depth and meaning that may enrich your life, so that you discover if there really is a Divine Oneness to life that can be authentically lived.

*　　*　　*

Exercise: believing in yourself

Allow yourself to become still. Take a little time to do this. Don't rush. When you are ready, start the following exercise.

1. Be aware of the chair you are sitting on and aware of your body. Be aware that your body is in contact with the space around you. As you do so, allow yourself to generate a sense of presence. Be present to yourself in the moment and realise that by acknowledging your body, your thoughts and your feelings, you are acknowledging who you are. Take a few moments to be present to your thoughts and yourself.

2. Now become aware of the breath. Allow your consciousness to be present with the in- and out-breath. Observe your breathing. As you breathe in, mentally repeat to yourself, 'I am this breath'. And as you breathe out, 'This breath I am'. Be aware of these thoughts as you breathe in and out. Do not try to control your breathing, but allow your breath to breathe you.

3. Now with every in-breath, repeat with feeling, 'I accept myself'. As you breathe out, repeat, I love myself'. Do this for about one and half minutes.

4. Next, breathe in and repeat, 'I am lovable'. And as you breathe out, repeat, 'I am loved'. Do this with feeling, knowing these statements are true. Do this for about one and half minutes.

5. Then breathe in and repeat, 'I respect myself'. Breathe out and repeat, 'I am respected'. Do this for about one and half minutes.

6. As you breathe in, say to yourself, 'I am one with God'. As you breathe out, repeat, 'God's oneness is part of me'. Do this for about one and half minutes.

7. Now, as you breathe in, repeat, 'I am one with the spirit world'. And as you breathe out, repeat, 'The spirit world is one with me'. Do this for about one and half minutes.

8. Next, breathe in with a sense of presence to the *now*, the present moment of your eternal existence and repeat, 'I am one with my mediumship'. As you breathe out, repeat, 'My mediumship is one with me'. Do this for approximately one and half minutes. Then be still for approximately two minutes and be aware of the deeper implications of these statements – that within you there is infinite potential that connects profoundly with the spirit world surrounding and working within and through you.

Know that your path will open before you and that you, God and the spirit world will walk together. Feel peace, confidence and trust flowing through you. Feel loved and an energizing healing presence flowing through you. Feel at one with all, with the spirit world and with everything that you are. Stay with these feelings for as long as you wish and blend with the spirit, God and your unique spirit Self. As you do this, notice any impressions or feelings that surface. Notice any changes in your perceptions and any changes within you that have been brought about or have started to unfold.

9. When you feel ready, allow yourself to return to your regular self with a sense of gratitude to all that has unfolded in this exercise. In your everyday life, honour all the seeds that you have planted in this meditation.

Expanding
our Awareness

7

❖

Like most people I have often found myself attracted to the natural world and its beauty. But as I pursued the development of mediumship, I began to notice differences in the way a tree, bush or flower in the countryside or a town park affected me to such a degree that when I look at and reflected upon it, I found myself becoming still within and aware of states of being that are hard to express in words.

Through this stillness and awareness I noticed that my outer perceptions changed. I would become completely enraptured by what I was contemplating. Somehow I knew that here within a living expression of Nature was God's presence. I don't know how I knew this, but I felt as though I had always known it somehow.

As I developed my mediumship and travelled more extensively in the UK and abroad, I began to notice how Nature affected me in different ways and started to realise its importance. I began to appreciate the sacredness of life much more than before and found this sacred presence in all things and species. This also included a deeper appreciation of the things our human species had created because of the creative mind that had produced them. In the course of my development I have come to realise how our individual spirit, Nature, the spirit world and God are continuously creating, and how by participating with this activity we become co-creators with the creative powers of all life.

Embracing all

When we embrace all existence, our lives become richer. Life on Mother Earth is not a negative place that we feel we would be only too pleased to escape. Her beauty inspires awe and wonder and has great healing qualities.

All life is sacred and ultimately derives its existence from God. We therefore need to seek to become one with this sacredness that exists in everything and everyone and respect and care about all life, including ourselves. Anything that separates us from others means separating ourselves from life and the awe inspiring creativity of God and spirit working through all.

By deepening our understanding we realise that all is interconnected and are parts of one great ocean of life. Here we find a level of our being in serene balance with all. It is only the appearance of separation from this reality – created by restrictive thoughts, emotions and perceptions – that stops us recognising and manifesting it and allowing it to have more influence on our lives.

The choices we have

In the process of unfoldment a particular area to consider is to do with choice and how to integrate the things that open to us as we move forward, such as a fuller understanding of spiritual principles and the implications behind spirit communication and how these can widen our perceptions and influence our everyday actions.

It is also essential in our unfoldment to understand the implications of the law of cause and effect: *as we think and act, so we become*. We need to understand how this leads us to express the law of association and examine this law in our lives, how we think, how our thoughts connect us with various levels of experience and see if this is helping us awaken to our spiritual consciousness. Is this helping us to associate with God and Nature and to realise the oneness of all things?

Harmonising the whole

Unfoldment and awareness are about spiritualising and harmonising every level of our being: body, mind, feelings, emotions, psyche and spirit. We cannot have a philosophy for life unless we allow all of human experience to be a part of it and develop through this ideas that form the basis for how we live.

This needs to be based on fully and wholesomely living our lives the best we can and discovering what is individually suitable for our growth. It means we do not accept things blindly but discover for ourselves what is right or wrong, just or unjust, and have the courage and conviction to follow our own paths and continually find spiritual truths for ourselves.

Living by spiritual laws means going beyond ordinary laws, taking responsibility for every area of our lives – our thoughts, feelings and actions – and being respectful of everyone and every form of life with which we come into contact. We may not be able to accomplish this overnight, but it is in the trying that we become more caring, loving, centred, responsible and empowered spiritual beings.

Powers of stillness and awareness

By sitting regularly and being still we learn how to enter a state of inner silence that leads to knowledge of our authentic spirit Self. Through embracing this intrinsic part of ourselves we awaken to something that can transform our whole being and give our lives more meaning, purpose and direction.

If awareness is healthily maintained, it will open new doors in our unfoldment. By using it to investigate and increase our spiritual and psychic knowledge we can grow in wisdom and understanding and awaken our lives to greater possibilities. In the beginning stages our mind may be more familiar with everyday knowledge and thought rather than spiritual perceptions of life. We may feel as Shakespeare described it, like 'a stranger in a strange land', and be unsure about our abilities, as we often limit ourselves and underrate what we can truly achieve in life and our development.

It is only through awareness of and creatively working with our thoughts, feelings and emotions that we manifest more positive qualities within us and embrace new realms of being. Through becoming increasingly aware of our actions and reactions we become more spiritually responsible and find the direction we need to move forward. Until we have awakened to self-awareness we can never truly know who we are and fully trust ourselves.

We see that self-awareness and awareness of our true spirit Self are not about limited ideas of spiritual and psychic unfoldment, but the whole of what we are and the whole of an abundant and authentic life.

The spirit seeking expression

Deep intuitive wisdom that can guide us in our lives takes time and patience to develop and requires us to cultivate various powers such as reflective reasoning, knowledge based on experience and an acceptance of things as they really are.

Life is always about moving on and evolving in the eternity of existence, and each of us needs to face each moment, each passing phase of life with wisdom, acceptance and compassionate understanding. We are all imbued with intuitive abilities, but we need wisdom and compassion as well in order to be able to reflect and learn from various situations encountered in life and to act in skilful ways that benefit not only ourselves but also others.

There is no point in living with regrets if things have not turned out as we feel they should, as the past has gone and the only thing that can be changed is how we respond to and are influenced by the past in the present moment.

We must try at all times to cultivate an awareness of and a creative responsiveness to new events and any previously undiscovered potential that may unfold. We are infinite and because we are infinite we obviously have no beginning or end. Our beginning-less and endless Self does not need to view life as missed opportunities but seeks to call us to ways in which it can skilfully manifest its true nature, its Divinity, more purely in every moment.

Human qualities and spiritual actions

When we look at the lives of some of the great masters of spirituality – those that have brought about great changes or have profoundly influenced people's lives – no matter how advanced we might consider them to be, we ought to never lose sight of the fact that they still have human qualities. ('Keep me away from the wisdom which does not cry, the philosophy which does not laugh', the mystical poet Kahlil Gibran said.) Invariably, they are not people who could be described as placid, but have been people of action, social change and profound teachings. It is their sense of humanity and human justice that often spurred them on to do great things and impart exceptional wisdom.

Sometimes we think of spirituality in terms of idealistic routes of expression that do not allow for the complexities of existence and the many different facets of a person's life. There are often reasons why we sometimes act less than we feel we could. This is why great teachers such as Jesus taught that we should not judge lest we be judged. 'Never judge someone until you have walked a thousand miles in his or her shoes' as the Chinese saying goes.

* * *

Exercise: blending with the spirit, healing your life and awakening to your own spirit

Do not rush this practice, but allow yourself time to stay with it for as long as it feels comfortable. Start slowly. Then add the five steps gradually, stage by stage, when you feel ready to move through them.

1. Become still and quiet. Allow yourself to enter into the stillness. Let everything become quiet within you, but without forcing yourself to be still. As you become aware of the stillness and quietness, listen to it.

Allow it to speak the language of your heart. Just become still, then allow yourself to become aware of how greatly loved you are by the unseen world of the spirit and are a part of the spirit's creative power. Allow your awareness of this to intensify and deepen. Stay aware of this and try not to drift away from it. Become aware of the love that is flowing through you – through your body, mind and spirit.

2. Recognise that this love has the power to heal the whole of your physical being, all the pain and disturbances in your life that connect with both the past and the present. And as it flows through you, it will seek to show you how greatly loved you are. It seeks to encourage you to learn how to love yourself, to accept yourself, to be compassionate towards yourself, to be forgiving of your faults. It also seeks to encourage you to love all life.

Through this love you will learn to forgive those who may have hurt you. As you do this, allow your mind to become free, to become accepting of all that has happened to you. Realise that you have learned about life in all dimensions and this learning has helped you to be a more compassionate and understanding person who is moving forward on a spiritual quest.

3. As the love and healing flows through you, notice how it harmonises your body and mind and brings about a deeper feeling of freedom. Notice how this is helping you to discover the power and the potential that your spirit possesses. Feel the love bringing healing into every aspect of your being, into every relationship that you have with life, with the world around you and within you. Be aware that this power and love and healing connects to the spirit world.

As you seek this blending of yourself and the whole of your being with the world of the spirit, stay with what it reveals and let its presence build. Be open and willing for communication to come, knowing that you are sitting in the power of your own being and the power of the spirit world that has made its presence known – that it journeys with you and is always there, and seeks to encourage you to find freedom and achieve the best in your life.

4. Bring your hands up and cross them over your heart and be aware for a few moments of a healing power flowing through you, around you and within you. Feel it flow through the world (of which you are a part) – both seen and unseen – and feel its power of love flowing to those with whom you a have deep affection and to those you may dislike and to all life.

5. Be still before returning to yourself, knowing that you have brought about great changes that will always be with you.

The Divine
Spirit

8

❖

There is something within each of us which knows that it is more than the body. We can term this state of knowing as being a high form of intuition. Its unfoldment can be likened to an echo of the spirit, something within our consciousness that keeps endeavouring to bring to the surface of our minds a higher sense of being.

When this level is awakened to, we experience the Divine's creativity expressing itself in and through our world and the Universe. We discover unity with all life and through this unity inspiration flows as a creative force. This awakening leads us to knowing our authentic Self – to the Divine Spirit Self that transcends and also connects us with all. It leads us to the God Self, which is both Mother and Father and the eternal good that exists in all things.

When we come to this state of knowing and being, we start to ask age-old questions about who we are, where we are going and what is creating the appearance of separation from our authentic spirit nature.

Becoming more receptive

If we truly wish to develop and manifest all that is good within us, we need to harmonise our lives with the spirit. If we accept there is a part of us that never dies, then we need to integrate this knowledge into our lives, investigate its implications and establish greater awareness of its reality in our unfoldment. As we open to our eternal Self (the spirit that we are, which is an individual expression of the supreme

Spirit) and to the Spirit that permeates all, various changes will begin to take place. We will become more aware of the invisible world of the spirit and its influence and of various responsibilities that are essential for following spiritual paths. We will then find ourselves responding to the Divine and the spirit world's influence with more receptivity.

Never lose sight of the fact that the Divine Spirit is constantly seeking to refine the finite and to express itself more harmoniously through all. This is why awareness, compassion and wisdom are key areas of spirituality as they lead us to purer states of being, knowing and interaction with the Divine in everyday life. For our true spirit Self is whole and without boundaries and continuously seeks to express this wholeness and boundless nature in and through every level of our being and everything that we do.

It knows no limitations and has the power to bring about positive changes, congruence in the ways we think, feel and act and enhance all creative abilities and qualities of compassion we have.

Acknowledging the power within

To trust the power of the spirit within is to realise that it can only create good and therefore there is nothing to fear and everything to attain by opening to its infinite life affirming possibilities. The more receptive we are to the spirit Self's presence, the more freedom we find in everyday life and the truer we will be to ourselves and others. The universal mind and consciousness of the Divine will function in a less restrictive way within us, through us, as us. We will acknowledge the work of the Divine as an essential part of our own being and how it connects us with all creative activity. Through this we become finer instruments for the work of the spirit and less inhibited by the appearance of everyday restraints of life and living.

Beyond boundaries

At an ultimate level we are not human beings unfolding to spiritual experience, but spiritual beings experiencing human realms of existence.* This points to something within human experience that is evolving through the activity of a spiritual force. For the Hindu, the Christian, the Muslim, the Sikh and the people of the Jewish faith, it may be termed as God or the Divine. For the Buddhist it will be described as Nirvana, beyond description, forms and concepts, as a state of no mind, pure unconditioned awareness, emptiness, neither being nor non-being, or as the spiritual core of all: our ever-present Buddha Nature.

Many of the teachings I have looked at and spiritual teachers I have had the privilege to have worked with and met have awakened within me an ongoing search to discover and find ways that can best unfold experiences that go beyond boundaries. Such teachings and people have brought about a growing awakening to how we are capable of great acts of compassion and kindness, and can communicate with and be influenced by realms beyond physical levels of knowing

*This sentence is from the conversations with Glyn that were done for the *Realms of Wondrous Gifts* book, and shows him referring to and paraphrasing a popular saying that is often accredited to Teilhard de Chardin.

to realising there is an ultimate deathless, sacred and eternal reality permeating all – something that is paradoxically both immanent and also transcendent. This takes us beyond the normal seeing, feeling and hearing states of mediumistic and psychic awareness to an understanding of there being a profound presence within all.

Limitless potential

The highest principle in all life is the Spirit and it is this which gives life to physical form. It is the eternal 'I', the God within and links us with the creative principle in all. It is the authentic Self, our original goodness, which seeks to encourage us to evolve and provide us with limitless potential at every level of our being. We therefore need to try in our unfoldment to understand this higher aspect of ourselves and observe how it functions through and can influence us. When we awaken to the spirit within, as well as the One Spirit in all life, we open ourselves to a variety of possibilities and experience.

It is by refining our perceptions and opening our minds that the authentic spirit Self's presence becomes more noticeable and life takes on greater meaning. As we awaken to its influence, we open to our own innate wisdom and gain insight into the reality of the spirit. We start to see the world and our place in it from a more positive and altruistic perspective and awaken to the true 'I' consciousness within.

This happens because of an increased awareness of our psychic sensitivity. We discover things such as Nature, beauty and everyday activity beginning to have a more profound effect upon us and find all life and experience drawing us to deeper levels of understanding. Through this we discover the Divine Spirit in all, as well as the good in all and our view and experience of everyday life shifts to harmonious perspectives. All life and experience become the substance for growth and reflection and parts of spiritual unfoldment. We gradually awaken and take responsibility for what is happening within and around our lives, and make changes that bring us closer to a spiritual way of life and living.

A greater life

We live, move and have our being in God. We came from and are a part of God. The very foundations of our lives belong to God. It is the substance, continuity and activity of all life. We derive everything from God. Our mind is God's altar, our body is its temple and our spirit is God's home. All creative potentials and possibilities are within this spirit that we are, which connects us deeply with the creativity of the Divine in all life.

We need to be conscious that it is through our minds, emotions and individuality that we develop the ability to be more Divinity-centred and establish greater awareness of who we are and how we are interconnected with everything and everyone. The more we are able to recognise this reality, the more receptive we will be to infinite qualities of good within us. This will give us the strength to free our minds and emotions and embrace a greater truth to live by.

Manifesting our spirit Self

Instead of being bound by the appearance of separation from God and our true spirit Self, we need to find ways of freeing our minds and emotions and embracing a life of truth, harmony, love, joy, peace, openness, unity and compassion.

Through this we discover that nothing is worth doing unless it has a spiritual basis for growth and good in our lives and in the world, and how both growth and goodness are intrinsic facets of God interacting with and expressing goodness through us. So let us make our actions at one with our minds and hearts, and our minds and hearts at one with God, so that the spirit that we are may allow its radiance to shine and manifest more purely in our everyday lives.

It is through the process of self-realisation that we grow to accept our individual selves as spirit and recognise that this real Self has its being in something even greater – a power that is all-loving, understanding and permeates all. We begin to acknowledge that what God is, we are – that our individual selves are expressions of the Divine, and that God is continuously expressing goodness and creativity in and through everything and everyone.

By awakening to this reality, we discover a myriad of positive qualities within us. Unfoldment then becomes a matter of bringing these to the surface and allowing them to become profound influences that can guide us in our daily lives, which help us actualise the potential of inherent gifts of original goodness, such as creative, mediumistic and compassionate awareness and actions.

*   *   *

Exercise: practising affirmative prayer

Make a definite time, twice a day if possible, to be alone. Sit down and compose your mind and think about God. Try to arrive at a deep sense of peace and calm, then assume an attitude of trust in that great power that is God. Next say to yourself the following:

> *The words I speak express the law of goodness and will bring about positive growth, because they are operating on the creative power of God that is within me. Good alone goes from me and good alone returns to me.*

You are now ready to expand your positive affirmation. Begin by saying:

> *These words are for myself (speak your name). Everything I say is for me and about me. It is the truth about my real Self (think about your spiritual nature, the Divine reality of yourself – the God in you).*
>
> *I know that God is the eternal source of goodness, light, love, wisdom and truth. These attributes are mine now at this moment because these things of God are within me and God's creative power is within me. The God within is the giver and sustainer of all life. I know that I (repeat your name) receive from this great power of original goodness all*

that I need for my spiritual journey. My every need is met now (state your needs).

I let go of all negative thoughts – I release them. I let go of all negative emotions – I release them. I let go of all doubts about myself and my pathway in life – I release them. I know that God and the spirit will guide and direct me to make the right decisions in life. I give thanks and so it is.

Statements such as this are not so much instructions to God, but are positive affirmations that remind us that God is limitless and is expressing itself as our individualised spirit and through us that self-same limitlessness. The more open we are to the Divine's influence, the more responsive we will be to gifts such as kindness, compassion, friendship and living in harmony with all. This operates through the universal law of cause and effect: *as we think, so we become.*

This statement can be seen as true in various areas of our lives. If we are little-minded, we receive little in return. If we are loving, we will attract love. If we are hateful, we shall attract hate. Laughter attracts more laughter. Joy attracts more joy and so on. So let us be realistic and honest with ourselves and remember that both God and spirit seek to encourage us to embrace the life we were born to live. Let us then be greater-minded and open-hearted that we may awaken to greater things.

Appendix I
*Deeper Dimensions of Mediumship**

Mediumship's prime aim is of course to prove survival after death of the physical body. But is this *the whole* of what mediumship is about? If all life, including not only realms of human life but also the natural world – of which we are a part – are expressions of the spirit, it then follows that it would be beneficial to expand our understanding of the spirit world in order to awaken to other spheres of awareness that link us profoundly with life and its evolvement.

In the light of such an inclusion and awareness, I feel it is important to reassess the central core of mediumship

---

*This is a transcribed and reworked edited version of a dictated article Glyn did on 1st January 2013. Psychic News published an edited version of it from a quickly done cut-down first draft of Glyn's words that was sent to them, under the title *Deeper Dimensions of Development*. The above uses the original title Glyn gave it, as well as extra material and alternative edited extracts to PN's version, from the much longer original article Glyn dictated.

It should be mentioned that transcribing spoken words into written sentences is more of an art of capturing key points of what someone said and their distinctive choice of terms and phrases, and putting them into coherent grammatical form without unnecessary repetition, instead of simply typing out word-for-word the way that things were said. Some linking phrases have been added in places in order to introduce or join passages or refer back to a previous point made for the purpose of helping the reading flow and gel as a unified article.

so it not only includes messages of human survival but explores other essential fields of unfoldment. I am thinking here of areas which are not just message or human focused but encompass more than mediumistic and human life. For I believe that without this wider embrace, it will be difficult to move healthily forward in our development.

The message of the spirit

If we look at the early years of modern Spiritualism, we find accounts of spirit communicators bringing not only messages about continuous human progression and survival but also seeking to encourage a recognition of the profound unity we have with *all people* and *all life*.

Many reports of early spirit communicators show them focusing on wide topics of spirituality, and displaying a deep interest in Earth's physical evolvement, as well as human ideas and beliefs – spiritual, religious, social, scientific, and political – and how these affect us. They displayed an awareness of how some nations developed a false sense of human, religious and/or racial superiority and how such things are harmful, as they cause an unhealthy separation between people and promote a separation of humans from the natural world.

If we consider how there are still growing divisions in the world and a rise in environmental damage, we as representatives of the spirit need to consider working against such activities and consider promoting the unity that is recognised and propounded by the spirit.

Ultimately there is no true separation between people

and other life, either in this life or after physical death. We are essentially one spirit that is without boundaries and interconnected equally with all.

These deeper dimensions of spirituality and mediumship require us to work healthily on ourselves in order to overcome limiting perceptions and cultivate an openness that is capable of embracing our true being and spiritual potential so they can be realised, embodied and wholesomely expressed. Spirituality and mediumship, their development and unfoldment, need to be understood as paths for bringing about these changes of perception that awaken us to wholesome transformation.

Until such a healthy stage of attunement is established, we will obviously not be able to implement and live deeper levels of unfoldment. In order to reach such a stage, we need to look at what is happening within our lives and our psychological selves, as both spirituality and mediumship connect with the mind and the whole of our existence, and are influenced by and expressed through numerous levels of life and experience.

If we allow it, mediumistic phenomena will seek through the deeper levels of our being to bring about changes in our perceptions, beliefs and any inhibiting qualities we have. Though it should be mentioned that this happens without demand, as the choice and responsibility for embracing such changes are left up to us to make.

Healthy approaches

Healthy approaches to mediumship are about considering whether we are merely the products of others who may have trained, spoken and/or lectured to us about its unfoldment, and what it does or does not include. As no two people are the same, no two people's paths will ever be identical. What might be beneficial for one person, might not be for another.

From my experience as a teacher I have found it helpful to examine things from the individual perspectives of my students and to encourage them to explore their own experiences, strengths, interests, knowledge and potential in order to discover their own insights about their growth. Through this they develop their mediumship in openly unique ways that do not require them to leave things out that they may hold as important such as other fields of knowledge, development and spirituality.

Instead of being restricted by aims to make everyone work, think and teach in the same way, which is psychologically unhealthy, they are able to become mediums and teachers that embrace more inclusive realms of activity. I make this point because of concerns I have about focusing *solely upon* human survival to the exclusion of other fields of development and the oneness and survival of *all life* and the responsibilities we share for the welfare and harmony of all.

When we look deeply into mediumship, we discover that it in fact connects with numerous spheres of existence. The spirit world permeates all, not merely spirit communication. Of course, there are different opinions people have, but an acceptance of difference is not the same as promoting a one cap fits all ideal.

Because mediumship touches every level of human life, the spirit world is interested in the welfare – mentally, physically and spiritually – of the whole of our being and the whole of our Earth life. For I have often noticed, which I'm sure the early pioneers of Spiritualism must have also observed, those in the spirit world endeavouring to make us aware of how interrelated and interested they are in all levels of existence.

Ongoing unfoldment

Central principles within different branches of Spiritualism need to be examined in the light of individual experience and contemporary understandings about life and living. Some principles are universal and have been taught since the earliest days of spiritual insight such as compassion, unity in diversity, and kindness to other people and species. However, some principles may need to change with time as new wisdom about spirituality, creation, life and the psychological make-up of our being are discovered.

Because of this, we will need to turn our attention within and look within our mediumistic and spiritual growth at the development of our beliefs and understanding about unfoldment. This naturally encourages us to be open to numerous possibilities of potential and nurturing change, spiritual maturity, and embracing teachings that are relevant to our current age.

Within this, we can look at what the deeper levels of spiritual insights and mediumship can encourage, not only within ourselves but also others. For me, mediumship is not just a gift or an ability but a sacred vocation. This sacredness, I feel, needs to become the foundation of all that we strive for in life. It isn't necessarily about being religious or about beliefs, but basing our unfoldment on experience and an authentic understanding of what mediumship can truly mean in the here and now of contemporary life.

Through such understanding we may then, with open minds, allow ourselves to present the intention to serve the spirit world in the truest ways we can. And within this, we can then allow ourselves to become more aware of the harmony and interconnectedness that exists in all – to allow for *the spirit in all* to inspire us and express possibilities of awakening that are within us and all things at all times.

Appendix II
*The Creative Teacher, the Unfolding Student**

O ne obstacle that is often encountered in teaching mediumship is that some students have already made up their minds about its development, which then makes it difficult for experienced teachers to share their insights and experience. Another problem is when teachers themselves impose their own ideas about development without first investigating what is happening with the student and seeing what the best way forward is for any potential medium. Middle ground invariably needs to be found for the spirit to bring forth their influence and wisdom.

Unfoldment is really about an ongoing discovery of the spirit world, consciously seeking help from the spirit, how to creatively co-operate with them, and realising how our unfoldment can enhance any abilities we have. I believe it is important to practise this art of creative co-operation

---

*This is a transcribed and reworked edited version of a dictated article Glyn did on 1st January 2013. Psychic News published an edited transcript of it from a quickly done cut-down first draft of Glyn's words that was sent to them. The above uses extra material and alternative edited extracts to PN's version, from the much longer original article Glyn dictated.
   The note from Appendix I about transcribing spoken words into written sentences also applies to this article.

and blending with the spirit world in order to build an ongoing healthy development. This is why we need to be mindful and aware of any experiences that manifest within our mediumship – from the perspective of feeling, inner knowing, inner hearing and seeing – and to investigate how the manifestation of these experiences affect our consciousness. Through this investigation we begin to bring about and notice patterns of change that affect both our inner and outer awareness of life and development.

We must remember that not only our inner senses – mediumistic, psychic and spiritual – but that our physical senses which have wondrously taken millions of years to evolve are equally valid, as spirituality is not an escape from one world into another but an inclusion of the whole of life. What is reflected upon inwardly, will manifests outwardly and vice versa. We therefore need to look at ourselves both inwardly and outwardly to see how all of our senses can lead us to essential dimensions of mediumship and spirituality.

If truly embraced, this can then lead to recognising and honouring not only the sacredness of our own existence but all life – human and non-human realms of activity – and awakening to lasting healthy stages of unfoldment. It involves opening to new experience and understanding profound changes that can, if we are willing to allow it, be integrated and authentically lived in our lives.

When we look into realms of mediumistic phenomena, we need to be aware that our minds, beliefs and ideas will affect and colour mediumistic abilities. This is why it is important to question how open we are to the spirit, their influence and knowledge. By continually reflecting and wholesomely working on our unfoldment, we can become more receptive to the spirit's guidance and wisdom.

Working with students

It is obviously important for teachers of mediumship to have a clear understanding of what it involves. An open awareness is needed to assess the extent to which students can touch levels of mediumistic unfoldment – to assess ways in which spirit communicators work with each student and make themselves uniquely known. It is crucial to link in and support students when they are exploring their unfoldment in order to see how evidence of survival is being established, what it means and how it influences potential mediums.

The teacher's role is to suggest, without imposing rigid rules, ways that students can move forward with open receptivity. In short, I believe it is important for teachers to encourage students to look to those that work with them in the spirit world as their ultimate guides for their unfoldment. Teachers are merely there to support them in this exploration and discovery. By encouraging this and establishing close union with the spirit world, a freer and more open form of mediumship reveals itself.

Keeping the doors open

Ultimately, mediumship and its phenomena cover vast plateaus of awareness and potential. I personally feel there are still realms of phenomena that we have not yet fully awakened to or even begun to discover. But one concern I have is imposing *rigid* beliefs about things that may have worked for others in the past being seen without question as right for students today, as we will be in danger of closing doors on new discoveries and experience. I'm not suggesting that we throw the baby out with the bath water but pointing out that we need to be aware that mediumship is an individual experience that never unfolds in exactly the same way for everyone. And just as God is continuously creating and life is evolving, we also need to be forever moving forward and be wisely creative in the present.

In its deepest sense, mediumship awakens us to clear seeing, to an intelligent world of spiritual insights. Of course there are 'beginning stages', which can in fact be encountered *at any point* in development, where things do not fall into place, appear to go wrong and new learning is needed. Nonetheless, it is by exploring, instead of rejecting, different and difficult stages of growth with wise understanding that firmer ground is established and authentically achieved. Yet within this unfoldment, it is important to realise that both worlds of activity – the world of the medium and the communicating spirit – are still evolving and experimenting.

Deeper attunement

The prime purpose of mediumship is to prove survival after death of the physical body. But we need to remember that people come to mediums with different expectations and levels of doubt about what they consider as evidential.

If mediums are influenced by such things, it can consciously or unconsciously leave the door open to manipulating information from the spirit world to fit with sitters' expectations.

We also need to consider how we are both finite and infinite, and what this implies. Spiritual teachings often highlight how we are essentially a spirit with a body – that we are in fact already living in a spirit world – and how our perceptions simply need to open in order to discover this truth for ourselves. Mediumship is therefore not about trying to go someplace else but about awakening to what is already a part of our being – to realise that we are *already* profoundly interwoven with the spirit world, and how communication with the spirit takes place through this connection. It is because of this non-separateness that communicators are able to express their thoughts through us to impart information about survival and profound teachings to live by.

Embracing a greater whole

In teaching about mediumship, it is beneficial to take into account the sensitivity of everyone's being, including our own, and avoid putting areas of development into separate boxes as *everything* is interconnected and continuously interacting with everything else – physically, psychically and spiritually – and therefore not separate. Within this interrelated interaction, unhelpful restrictive realms of thought and perception will be problematic and will affect the progression of our potential and unfoldment. It is therefore important to observe what is going on in our lives and work on all things that can inhibit our growth.

Conclusion

Each of us is a unique part of life. For the brief time we are here on Earth we may see further than material egocentric life and recognise that we and all life are manifestations of an essential spiritual source.

Each of us, I believe, is here for a purpose. By taking responsibility for our development and discovering, through our own insights and experiences, the authentic nature of our being and the purpose of why we are here, we will recognise important life-changing dimensions of development, not only from mediumistic perspectives but also spiritual, psychological and human ones. Through this we discover what an all-encompassing spiritual life can truly entail.

So are you willing to embrace what may be currently unknown to you but if searched can be brought into being to enrich your life in wondrous ways? Hopefully your answer is an affirmative 'Yes'.

Sources

All chapters, the appendices and the first three quotations are from the below sources by Glyn Edwards, though some editing was done in places by Glyn and the compiler. Page numbers starting and ending in different places indicate where selected passages can be found, but do not imply the text was used in its entirety from one page to another.

Beginning and Biography Quotations
1st quote: *Realms of Wondrous Gifts*, p.108 (published 2008 and 2012).
2nd quote: *The Spirit World in Plain English*, p.15 (published 2011 and 2012).
3rd quote: From an interview with Glyn (February 2012).

Chapter 1: Realms of Unfoldment
Selections from two interviews with Glyn (January and February 2012).
Spirit Gems, p.58 (published 2011 and 2012).
The Spirit World in Plain English, p.69 (published 2011 and 2012).

Chapter 2: Sitting in the Power
Based on CD1 and from sleeve notes for
Merging with Spirit Consciousness (double CD, 2005).

Chapter 3: Psychic and Mediumistic Unfoldment
The Intuitive Arts (article extract, 2006).
Selections from an interview with Glyn (January 2012).
The Spirit World in Plain English, p.57-60, 68-69, 114-116
(published 2011 and 2012).

Chapter 4: The Mediumistic Journey
The Intuitive Arts (article extract, 2006).
Selections from an interview with Glyn (January 2012).
Realms of Wondrous Gifts, p.89-90, 97-98, 100-102, 106-108, 112-113
(published 2008 and 2012).
Spirit Gems, p.60, 70 (published 2011 and 2012).
The Spirit World in Plain English, p.15, 67, 113-114
(published 2011 and 2012).

Chapter 5: Developing Mediumistic Powers
Selections from an interview with Glyn (January 2012).
Spirit Gems, p.67, 70 (published 2011 and 2012).
The Spirit World in Plain English, p.77-80, 93-94, 98, 124
(published 2011 and 2012).

Chapter 6: The Spirituality of Mediumship
Dictated chapter by Glyn (February 2012).

Chapter 7: Expanding our Awareness
Selections from two interviews with Glyn (January and February 2012).
Realms of Wondrous Gifts, p.101-102, 111-115
(published 2008 and 2012).
Spirit Gems, p.69, 70, 73, 89 (published 2011 and 2012).

Chapter 8: The Divine Spirit
The Intuitive Arts (article extract, 2006).
Realms of Wondrous Gifts, p.95-96, 115 (published 2008 and 2012).
Spirit Gems, p.58-59, 63, 71-73 (published 2011 and 2012).
The Spirit World in Plain English, p.26-27, 59, 64
(published 2011 and 2012).

Appendix I: Deeper Dimensions of Mediumship
Dictated article (January 2013, edited extracts).

Appendix II: The Creative Teacher, the Unfolding Student
Dictated article (January 2013, edited extracts).

* * *

Note: *The Spirit World in Plain English* and *Spirit Gems* are thoroughly revised editions of earlier titles coauthored by Glyn Edwards and Santoshan that were republished in 2011 by S Wollaston and in 2012 by the Gordon Higginson Fellowship. *The Spirit World in Plain English* was first published by Quantum (an imprint of W Foulsham) in 1999 under the title *Tune in to Your Spiritual Potential*. *Spirit Gems* was also first published by Quantum and initially titled *21 Steps to Reach Your Spirit* in 2001 and later re-titled as *Unleash Your Spiritual Power and Grow* in 2007. The printed edition of *Realms of Wondrous Gifts* was first published by the Gordon Higginson Fellowship in 2008. Thoroughly revised and redesigned editions have since been published on both Amazon and Smashwords. Page numbers cited refer to the first printed edition although passages used for this book incorporate revisions made in later editions.

Afterword

Writing with Glyn by Santoshan/Stephen Wollaston

Shortly after I first met Glyn, a graphics partnership I had in London Docklands moved into computerised design work. I mentioned to Glyn that if he wanted to write and publish something, this was the time, as the technology made book-layout less expensive. As an energetic and creative young man as Glyn was, he instantly proposed that we write a book *together*, which I wasn't expecting, on different areas of spirituality and mediumship.

Glyn's input was amazing. He seemed to have no end of experience, wisdom and new perspective to add. Then synchronicity magically played a part when it was finished, as a call came through from the then editor of Psychic News, Tony Ortzen, scouting for a publisher, who asked Glyn if he would like to write a book. He quickly replied, 'Steve and I have just finished one'. We later revised and updated it in 2011 and gave it a more contemporary title than it previously had. Glyn was extremely pleased with the look and reading of the revised edition, which is clearly seen in his opening Acknowledgments.

After completing the first title, I had an idea for a workbook and this time approached Glyn about writing it together. We also revised and expanded it in 2011 and gave it a different title to what the previous publisher had given it. Once again, Glyn displayed how pithy he could be in putting great insights together. In the final section of the book, we found various quotations to put in on important spheres of unfoldment, which Glyn had no end of enthusiasm in finding key teachings from different writers and teachers he loved.

He then asked if I would put together a book on mediumistic and psychic powers in different traditions, as he wanted to promote a more inclusive and open-minded understanding of alternative paths amongst his students.

Having already written an article for an appendix that touched on this in a Yoga book with a swami, I accepted his request and expanded what I'd started in the other book but asked Glyn if he would also like to be interviewed for two large sections that could be included. He said he would. Questions put to him were invariably followed by a period of reflective silence. He would then answer fluently without pausing until he had covered all that he felt was needed to be said.

This anthology, *The Potential of Mediumship*, I suggested to Glyn about putting together. Glyn did a book launch for it after a truly dazzling public demonstration of his mediumship on 18th September 2012 at the Eastbourne Centre, East Sussex.

*   *   *

Reflections with Glyn Edwards, More Reflections, and the Complete Collection

Compiled and with Additional Material by Santoshan (Stephen Wollaston)

The *Reflections with Glyn Edwards* anthologies are full of wonderful quotations by Glyn for meditation and reflective purposes, and include additional passages by Glyn's long-time close friend Santoshan (Stephen Wollaston) from the books they worked on together and individually.

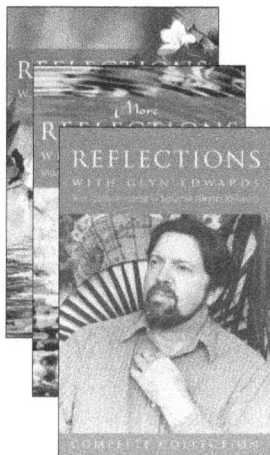

Mid-price paperbacks
142, 137 & 252 pages
ISBN 978-1080308798
ISBN 979-8397188913
ISBN 798860848986

Low-cost eBook editions available from Amazon and Smashwords. Hardback editions also available.

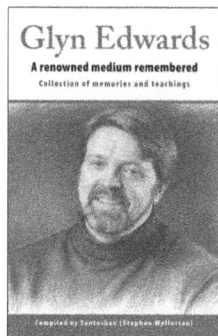

'His insight into and experience of an array of interrelated realms of spirituality was unquestionably phenomenal and deeply profound.'
~ From the compiler's introduction

Glyn Edwards
A Renowned Medium Remembered
~ Collection of Memories and Teachings
Compiled by Santoshan (Stephen Wollaston)

A unique collection of Glyn's inclusive wisdom on spiritual and mediumistic realms of unfoldment as well as a wonderful tribute book that honours his life and work. In this combined treasury of Glyn's teachings and memories about him, numerous insights and fond recollections are shared alongside various photographs. It includes a detailed biography about him, heartfelt stories by people whose lives he touched, and a collection of quotations, articles, workshop sections and exercises by Glyn, which give practical steps for awakening to the ever-present world of the spirit and the oneness of spiritual living.

118 pages with extra insde photos
ISBN : 978-0-9569210-4-8

eBook edition available from Amazon and Smashwords. Hardback edition also available.

'Many people are not aware how outstanding a medium and teacher Glyn in fact was... There are no adequate words to express the void that has been left without his physical presence.'
~ Ron Jordan (Devadūta), internationally renowned medium and spiritual teacher

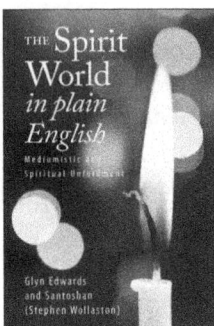

The Spirit World in Plain English
Mediumistic and Spiritual Unfoldment
Glyn Edwards and Santoshan (Stephen Wollaston)
Foreword by Don Hills

160 pages
ISBN 78-0-9569210-0-0

eBook edition available from Amazon and Smashwords. Hardback edition also available.

The Spirit World in Plain English is a revised and updated edition of the authors' first book. In this beneficial manual, Glyn Edwards and Santoshan share practical exercises and teachings for discovering inherent mediumistic and spiritual potential. Together, they combined their knowledge in far-reaching ways and cover numerous essentials for understanding and interacting with the ever-present world of the spirit.

'This book is more than just another book on spiritual and psychic development; it's literally the bible on development.'
~ Amazon UK (customer review of first edition)

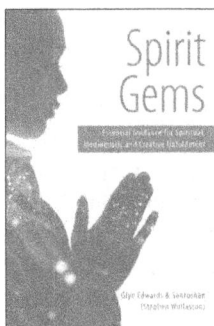

Spirit Gems
Essential Guidance for Spiritual, Mediumistic and Creative Unfoldment
Glyn Edwards and Santoshan (Stephen Wollaston)

128 pages
ISBN 978-0-9569210-1-7

eBook edition available from Amazon and Smashwords. Hardback edition also available.

Spirit Gems is a revised and expanded edition of the authors' second book, which provides practical steps for discovering how to live more freely, deeply and peacefully. Glyn Edwards and Santoshan write beautifully whilst covering essentials such as living in the now, facing our fears, finding unity with all, and harmonising the whole of ourselves. Both authors share profound insights for immersing our lives in spiritually and mediumistically centred living, which weave skilfully through various enriching realms of transforming experience.

'A must for anyone's bookshelf.'
~ The Greater World Newsletter
(review of first edition)

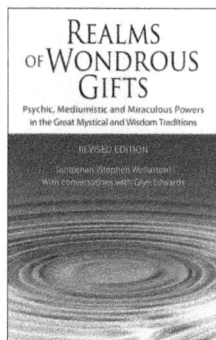

Realms of Wondrous Gifts
Psychic, Mediumistic and Miraculous Powers
in the Great Mystical and Wisdom Traditions
(revised and redesigned edition)
Santoshan (Stephen Wollaston)
With conversations with Glyn Edwards

Realms of Wondrous Gifts presents an in-depth look at psychic, mediumistic and miraculous powers in the world's great mystical and wisdom traditions, and includes key insights into various teachings and practices. It also includes two extensive conversations with Glyn Edwards, in which he eloquently shared far-reaching thoughts on several interwoven facets of development.

157 pages
ISBN 978-1658935630

Low-cost paperback and eBook edition available from Amazon and Smashwords. Hardback edition also available.

'A real gem of a book ... Highly recommended.'
~ Psychic World.

'A rare and enriching book.'
~ Eileen Davies, internationally renowned medium and spiritual teacher

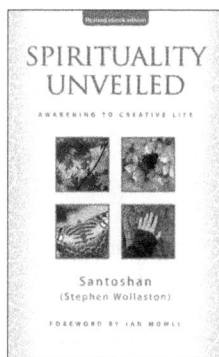

Spirituality Unveiled
Awakening to Creative Life
Santoshan (Stephen Wollaston)
Foreword by Ian Mowll

Spirituality Unveiled puts forward a succinct and compelling synthesis of numerous spiritual traditions. Whilst weaving together insights from contemporary and past masters of spirituality, along with holistic and Earth centred wisdom, it beautifully highlights teachings about the essentials of creative unfoldment and invites readers to join in the important search to find a healthy interaction with life.

144 pages
ISBN 978-1-84694-509-0

Low-cost eBook edition (which is shown above) available from Amazon and Smashwords.

'Integral thinking at its best ... a masterful synthesis.'
~ Marian Van Eyk McCain, editor of *GreenSpirit: Path to a New Consciousness*

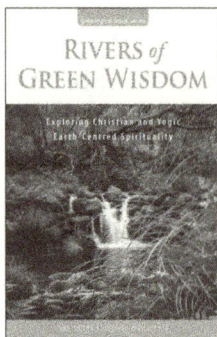

Rivers of Green Wisdom
Exploring Christian and Yogic Earth-Centred Spirituality
Santoshan (Stephen Wollaston)

In *Rivers of Green Wisdom* the author shares personal reflections on Christian, Yogic and Earth-centred wisdom and key stages encountered on his own spiritual journey. The book unveils central teachings about the sacredness of Earth and Nature, covers both past and present understanding about our interdependent relationship with the natural world, and how various teachers have looked for East-West fusions for deeper and more responsible living.

'Seldom do you find such practised clarity in revealing the wisdom of Spirit.'
~ Sky McCain, Vedantist and author of *Planet as Self: An Earthen Spirituality*

86 pages
ISBN 978-0-9935983-2-6

Low-cost paperback and eBook edition available from Amazon and Smashwords. Hardback edition also available.

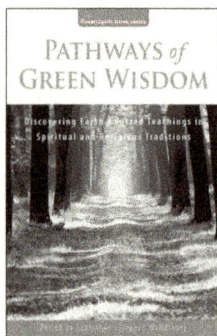

Pathways of Green Wisdom
Discovering Earth-Centred Teachings in Spiritual and Religious Traditions
Edited by Santoshan (Stephen Wollaston)

Pathways of Green Wisdom covers teachings and practices that promote honouring and compassionately caring for Nature. It brings together numerous reflective and informative pieces by contributors to GreenSpirit magazine spanning a period of 11 years, along with especially written new material. Contributors include progressive and insightful writers from various backgrounds. Each offers an enriching well to draw some nourishment and appreciate numerous Earth-centred dimensions of a particular spiritual path.

'This is a wonderful book, which takes you on a journey through various traditions.'
~ Ian Mowll, Interfaith minister and the coordinator of GreenSpirit

140 pages
ISBN 978-0-9935983-3-3

Low-cost paperback and eBook edition available from Amazon and Smashwords. Hardback edition also available.

The Varieties of Earth-Centred Practices
Eight Green Ways
Edited by Santoshan (Stephen Wollaston)

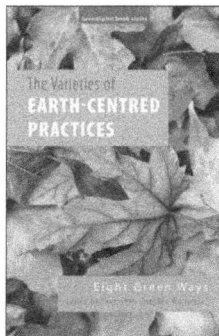

106 pages
ISBN 979-8305586718

Low-cost paperback and eBook edition available from Amazon and Smashwords. Hardback edition also available.

Covers eight interconnected key areas of Earth-centred wisdom: the Way of Simplicity, the Way of Storytelling, the Way of Creativity, the Way of Rambling, the Way of Gardening, the Way of Contemplation, the Way of Community, and the Way of Activism. Authors for each chapter write on and share their understanding of topics they are especially passionate about. Written by contemporary and former GreenSpirit trustees, the book is an insightful overview of different paths and experiences. It will inform you how living green means an array of practices that can overlap and bring meaning, purpose and healing to people's lives – bringing hope that is crucial for today's world and the health of our living planet and all life coexisting with Earth.

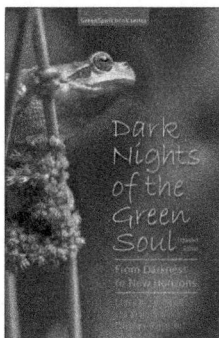

Dark Nights of the Green Soul
From Darkness to New Horizons
(expanded edition)
Edited by Ian Mowll and Santoshan (Stephen Wollaston)

148 pages
ISBN 978-1978414716

Low-cost paperback and eBook edition available from Amazon and Smashwords. Hardback edition also available.

Highlights insights about facing difficult times, alongside reflections on our interactive relationship with Nature. The book's four main parts present various perspectives about working with darkness and ways in which we can creatively move forward. It includes personal stories about times of difficulty people encountered, and explains how each of the storytellers found new meaning and growth by either connecting with an animal friend or in Gaia-centred spiritual awakenings and teachings.

'*Dark Nights of the Green Soul* is a compact, intelligent and highly accessible addition to the GreenSpirit Book Series.'
~ Chris Holmes, GreenSpirit council member

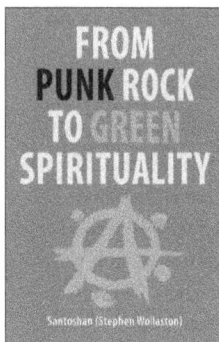

From Punk Rock to Green Spirituality

Santoshan (Stephen Wollaston)

A collection of eleven articles by the author, which include Caring for Our Sacred Earth, Awakening to Creative Life, Celebrating Our Interconnectedness with Nature, A Postmodern and Age-old Wisdom of the Heart, and Expanding Our Circle of Awareness.

104 pages
ISBN 9798511082547
Low-cost paperback and eBook.

The House of Wisdom
Yoga Spirituality of the East and West

Swami Dharmananda and Santoshan (Stephen Wollaston)
Foreword by Glyn Edwards

The House of Wisdom covers starting out and challenges on the spiritual path, and the Yogic understanding of our authentic Self.

'A real treasure-house of spiritual knowledge.'
~ Julie Friedeberger, author of *The Healing Power of Yoga*

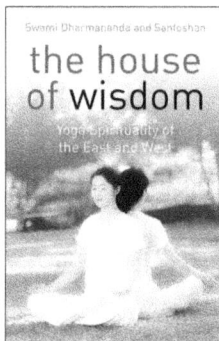

224 pages
ISBN 978-1-846940-24-8

GreenSpirit Reflections

Compiled by Santoshan (Stephen Wollaston)

A meditations book of profound and inspiring quotations on green spirituality. Drawing from a variety of GreenSpirit publications, this little book of relections gathers together numerous key insights in nine essential categories that can be seen as the core of Earth-centred wisdom.

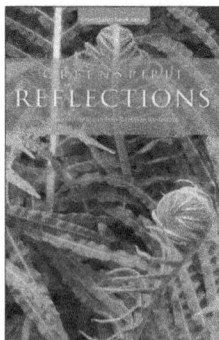

118 pages
ISBN 978-1-846940-24-8
Low-cost paperback and eBook.